Women In

Ministry

What Does the Bible Say?

By
Jacqueline T. Flowers

Foreword by
Jerry W. Flowers, Sr.

Llumina
Christian
Books

Additional Books Written By Dr. Flowers

Fashioned for His Glory
In His Presence
Where are the Men?
Woman Be Whole

Unless otherwise indicated, all scripture quotations are
from The King James Version of the Bible.

ISBN: 978-1-62550-394-7

Printed in the United States of America by Llumina Christian Books

Table of Contents

Dedication

This book is dedicated to every member of the Body of Christ. It is my sincere desire that this reading material will dispel much of the traditional error, which has poisoned the minds of people concerning Women in Ministry. I further pray that many women who have harbored the call of God within will be released to do all God has put in their hearts to do for His Glory.

One of the most powerful truths I have learned is, "We cannot change our lives, or how we think, until we change what we know." God's Word is made available to us in order that we know truth and order our lives thereby. Many people have a head knowledge of scripture, but no revelation. Revelation and insight come from God. We cannot attempt to interpret scripture in a surface manner. Neither can we attempt to study and rightly divide scripture by human intellect alone. The Bible is its own commentary and, if studied properly, the student will find that it interprets itself. It is incorrect to attempt to build a doctrine on a certain verse of scripture. Scripture must be interpreted in view of all the scriptures on that particular subject. God cannot and will not honor a misinterpretation of His Word.

Many people have read certain scripture passages within the Bible and attempted to build a doctrine without properly researching the scriptures thoroughly. There is a big difference in reading the Bible and studying the Bible. Reading is simply observing what is written for the purpose of absorbing information. However, studying is analyzing what is written for the purpose of absorbing understanding. Many have much information but no understanding of Biblical truth and history. This is one of the reasons there has been a perpetuation of the misinterpretation of scripture regarding the statement: "God does not use women to preach the gospel."

What Does the Bible Say?

When studying scripture for proper understanding and interpretation, we must consider who is being addressed, that is, who is God talking to, the custom of the day, the geographical and historical setting, the writer, the circumstances surrounding the writing and how it is relevant to us today. As we consider the scriptures concerning women in ministry, I understand that not every woman is called to the pulpit to preach the gospel publicly, but to those who have been yearning to glorify God because of the call, this book will bring freedom and encouragement. I encourage each woman to listen attentively to the Father's voice, harness your emotions and yield to the leading of the Holy Spirit. I pray every man who reads the book, will do so with a heart to receive and abandon all misinterpretation of scripture.

It is not God's will for any woman to sit aimlessly by, with a divine call to share the gospel, yet be unable to do so, because of the misinterpretation of scripture. Today is a new day. God is unveiling and revealing spiritual truth to all those who have ears to hear and hearts to receive. Surely He has something to say about the role women should fulfill in His Body.

I say to every woman, if God has called you to preach, or teach the gospel, He will make His will known to you as you search the scriptures and spend time in His presence. We cannot proclaim truth as female Pastors, without a ***divine call***. We cannot jump up and chose the pastorate as a career. This is a call initiated by an Almighty God, not man. He will prove you before all men. A woman's success as a woman in ministry is not dependent upon what others say or believe, but rather obedience to God, the proper heart attitude, discipline and consistency before God, dignity and the ability to be a serious student of the Word of God.

God is the only one who can initiate the call. He has reserved this right for Himself. It is imperative that we discern the voice of God. It is equally imperative that we never assume the role of Pastor, Teacher, or Evangelist, without expressed clarity from God. By this I mean, it is dangerous to launch into a work because of what we see God doing in and through others whom

ii

we admire. Without the grace of God and the anointing of God, we will ultimately fail in anything we attempt to do that God has not called us to do.

With the gift, God gives the measure of grace necessary to achieve every God-given assignment. Without the grace of God to fulfill the assignment, failure is imminent.

We must never assume we are called for a particular assignment; *we must know beyond any doubt*. God is obligated to make His plan and purpose for our lives crystal clear; otherwise, none of us could successfully establish order in this earth by fulfilling our God-ordained purpose. Once God speaks to us, He is great enough to confirm what He has said through our local pastors. Every believer must have a pastor.

If God has called you to the office of Pastor/Teacher, or Evangelist, allow God to groom you for the call. In the appointed time He will manifest Himself through you and all will know you are ordained of God. God told Joshua:

Joshua 3:7
This day will I begin to magnify you in the sight of all Israel, that the people may know that, as I was with Moses, so I will be with thee,...

There is an appointed season and when God is with you, He will endorse you before the world. I say to every woman, who is called of God, it is extremely vital that you are a member of a local church and that you have a Pastor who is thoroughly convinced that God is no "respecter" of persons. God will use your Pastor to feed you with knowledge and understanding **(Jeremiah 3:15)**. In the appointed season, God will confirm the call through your Pastor and you can go forth in ministry fully established, mature and balanced in all things, naturally and spiritually.

You can become all God has qualified you to be. He has deposited something of value within you and you are free in Him to "BE" all He says you are in His Word.

There still exist a few denominational groups who restrict women or only allow them to play a small role in their local assemblies because of their gender. Those who are truly called by God cannot be swayed by this. Just remain teachable and humble and trust God to elevate you in His own time.

Psalm 75:6-7

For promotion cometh neither from the east, nor from the west, nor from the south. But God is the judge: He putteth down one, and setteth up another.

Galatians 1:15-16

But when it pleased God, Who separated me from my mother's womb, and called me by His grace, To reveal His Son in me, that I might preach Him among the heathen; immediately I conferred not with flesh and blood:

Never have a pulpit mentality. By this I mean, don't get caught up in titles, positions and where you sit in the assembly. Titles, seats and positions do not validate the call. God validates the call and His validation is affected by the heart condition. Keep your heart pure of strife, envy, jealousy, competition, comparison, pride, greed and dissension. God will show Himself mighty on your behalf when your heart is perfect towards Him. **(II Chronicles 16:9)**

Finally, I dedicate this book to my husband, Reverend Jerry W. Flowers, Sr., whom God has used tremendously to prepare me for the Pastorate; my children, Demetrius, Tiana, and Jerry Jr.; to my mom, Betty L. Jackson, and dad, Doris Jackson, who are now in the presence of the Lord. I will forever thank God for them, their love, and the tremendous legacy they left me.

Foreword

The question, "Should women preach the gospel?" has been an issue of controversy for years. People have confined God to one gender for generations. If the earth-suit (flesh) is that of a male, many accept the fact that God can speak through him. However, if the earth-suit reflects one who is female we say, "Surely God can't speak through a woman." Even though God is the Creator of all mankind and He said, *"There is neither Jew nor Greek, there is neither bond nor free, there is neither male nor female: for ye are all one in Christ Jesus"* **(Galatians 3:28),** many are still limiting God to the method by which they feel He should operate in this earth.

I value Pastor Jacqueline T. Flowers as my wife, and as my Pastor, but I also value her as a woman chosen of God to declare the truth of the Gospel. I realize God is doing a great work in and through her. I see her as a pen in the hands of an Almighty God establishing order in this earth in the lives of many. As Joseph fully accepted the will of God for Mary, the mother of our Lord and Savior Jesus Christ, I fully accept the call of God upon her life and I will not allow anyone or anything to interrupt what God has called her to do. I release her to be all she can be to the Glory of God. God spoke to me concerning His will for her life and confirmed through me the call upon her life.

It is my desire that this book will enlighten many and encourage other men to accept the truth that God is God, and surely He can choose whomsoever He wills. As indicated in the dedication of this book, every scripture must be interpreted in light of what other scriptures say pertaining to the subject matter. It must harmonize with all scriptures.

Much error has resulted from many ignoring the law of scripture interpretation. How is it that many conclude that Paul was writing as inspired by the Holy Spirit, yet in the same breath, conclude that Paul in **I Corinthians 11:15,** tells women they can pray and prophesy, but in the 16th chapter he excludes them from ministering the Word of God? Something is innately wrong. There is clearly a contradiction here. However, it is not with the scripture, but rather the individual interpreting the scripture. The Bible does not contradict itself.

Careful study of Biblical history reveals why Paul made certain statements and to whom he was addressing when he made those statements. These issues will be explained in detail in this book. This book is written to bring clarity concerning many questions that have crippled many in the Body of Christ.

Much of what is said concerning women and their roles in the Body of Christ cannot be substantiated by scripture. Many verses have been taken out of context and interpreted incorrectly. These misinterpretations have caused many women to draw back from the call of God and many men to overlook the power of God flowing through many who are female in gender. Some are confused because they were told to never receive from women in ministry.

The misinterpretation of scripture has brought about spiritual bondage, and anything that subjects a person to bondage is not of God. I must emphasize that the Bible is truth without error. It is God's presentation of order for mankind in the family of God and in the home. It is its own commentary and will interpret itself if studied intently and properly and if the Holy Spirit is allowed to serve in His capacity as the Revealer of Truth. We must disregard preconceived ideas, pride, what others have said, traditional error and be willing to come into full knowledge.

God is God and He can use whomever He chooses to preach the "Gospel." We cannot disregard the gift of God in one who represents the female aspect of the Body of Christ. We must all be willing to receive God's Word regardless of whom He chooses to speak through. We cannot continue to allow a misinterpretation of scripture to pass on to other generations. The truth must be told today, and we must pass on sound doctrine with purity; uncontaminated by fleshly opinions and ideas.

Reverend Jerry W. Flowers, Sr.

Introduction

We are living during times when there is a greater awareness than ever before of the various roles women fulfill in the Body of Christ. Many women are operating in the office of Pastor/ Teacher, and Evangelist (Missionary). Despite the controversy and theological views many share concerning women Ministers, or Pastors, the numbers continue to escalate and many are flabbergasted.

The words documented by the Apostle Paul in **I Corinthians 14:34-35, I Timothy 3:1-2, and I Timothy 2:11-12**, have become the premise by which many condemn women who say they are called of God to preach, teach or pastor. We will examine these scriptures carefully to see what the Apostle Paul really meant. Was there intent on his part to establish a doctrine by which the entire Body of Christ should exclude women beyond his day from teaching, or preaching in the church? Is it the will of God for women to be silent in the church? Should a woman Pastor? Is every man the head of every woman? Who is the spiritual head of woman? Should a woman submit to every man? Should she submit to anything?

This book will reveal the heart of God concerning these issues and more. It amazes me that, in a universal sense, throughout the Body of Christ, the average church membership consists primarily of women. Women sing in choirs, give the announcements, lead devotion, and give a great percentage of their time and resources, not to mention their commitment to annual days and fund raising events.

How is it that women are known to be intense in prayer and the study of the scriptures, yet are forbidden by some to publicly instruct them in spiritual things? Something is innately wrong and it is my intention, as inspired by the Holy Spirit, to dispel the lies that have contaminated the thinking, attitude, and behavior of many in the Body of Christ and outside of the Body of Christ.

Religious indoctrination against women in the ministry is evident in the Body of Christ. Where did this religious indoctrination come from? The uneducated in spiritual matters, who in their own ignorance, have perpetrated a lie.

This book will unveil the truth and dispel the lies that have held people in spiritual ignorance concerning God's order for the Body of Christ and God's order for the home. After reading this book, you will be challenged to examine yourself, and embrace the truths outlined herein or reject them. Many will be brought to a point of repentance. To those who reject the truths presented, you will not be rejecting the vessel, but you will be rejecting Almighty God. I encourage you to be open to the Spirit of God as you read this book and be prepared to receive fresh illumination as He who is the "REVEALER" of Truth, expounds more perfectly on His purpose and plan for women in the "Household of Faith."

Examine the scriptures carefully and God will use the truths revealed in this book to minister to male and female alike. There will be no limit to what ministries will achieve when every member of the Body of Christ and every member of the family unit understand and operate by the order of God. Ignorance has hindered us for far too long. Religious and traditional error has hindered the progress of many ministries. I have also found that it is not only ignorance but the prideful and self-righteous attitude of many who would rather reject the truth than admit that they could have been wrong; or perhaps that they made a mistake concerning their interpretation of scripture. This self-righteous attitude and refusal to admit error have perpetuated many lies concerning women in ministry.

Paul was not married, but was assisted by women in ministry to fulfill his purpose. Man cannot reach maximum fulfillment and potential without woman. The fulfillment of God's plan, purpose and will for all mankind in this earth must be carried out by both genders, male and female.

Chapter One

Women in Ministry

Many would have us believe the Bible is a book which excludes women from leadership positions in the Body of Christ. Some are deceived and believe that only those who are male in gender must hold the positions of Pastor/Teacher, or Evangelist. Women preaching the Word of God in the local church has been viewed as a disgrace. It has been the belief of many that God has positioned the male gender to receive the blessings and gifts of an Almighty God free from the influence and wisdom of women. I must chuckle at this, because when God needed a vessel to establish His plan in the earth for the redemption of all mankind, He had to plant the seed of His Word in a woman. When Jesus got up out of the grave on Resurrection morning, it was a woman He told to tell the "good news", the gospel to His disciples. (**John 20:11-18**)

In the home, the roles of the husband and the wife have been misinterpreted. Perhaps, if I address history, I can clear up much misinterpretation of scripture during the times in which we live. In the Hebrew society, the husband was possessor and master of his wife, his children, his servants, his animals, and his property. The husband had the right to divorce his wife with little reason, although she had little or no redress if she were wronged by him. Absolute faithfulness was required of the wife, but not of the husband, so long as he did not violate the rights of another husband. Monogramy was and is the original plan of God. It speaks to the male man and the female man coming together under the authority of God in a governing institution called marriage. Two of the most powerful powerful words spoken by a husband and wife as "I Do!" Both are saying we will submit to God and we will submit to one another.

Genesis 2:24-25
Therefore shall a man leave his father and his mother, and shall cleave unto his wife, and they shall be one flesh. And they were both naked the man and his wife, and were not ashamed.

He could have as many wives as he wanted, but not the woman. Unfortunately, with this power and freedom, husbands began to abuse their authority in their households in the religious and social traditions of the family. Women were considered property and were demanded to obey their husbands, as domestic servants.

Those of us, who are serious students of God's Word, and who have experienced the burning fire of the call of God within, know that it is not God's order for man to oppress man in any form, whether male or female.

Genesis 1:26-27
And God said, Let us make man in Our image, after Our likeness: and let them have dominion over the fish of the sea, and over the fowl of the air, and over the cattle, and over all the earth, and over every creeping thing that creepeth upon the earth. So God created man in His own image, in the image of God created He him; male and female created He them.

Much of what we hear today concerning women is far from the truth. We fully understand that the role of women during the Old Testament and New Testament days was not typical and Jesus came to upset the order of the day. Many Biblical women in the Bible fulfilled roles that were subtle, quiet, and passive.

However, there are several occasions where women held powerful positions and often it was because of this, that many men were able to fulfill God's plan and purpose for their lives.

One instance involves a woman by the name of Deborah. During the time when Israel was ruled by Judges, Deborah was one of the thirteen judges. The word "judge" in the Hebrew is "shaphat" and it means to rule over; to govern; to oversee. She ruled over Israel for forty years and was known as a mother in Israel. (**Judges 5:7**) This woman ruled over a nation. She ruled as judge, over men and women alike. If God would use a woman to rule over a nation, surely he can use her to pastor a church. Deborah ruled when Israel was oppressed by Jabin, king of Hazor, and Sisera, the general of his powerful army. She was also a prophetess married to a man by the name of Lapidoth. The children of Israel would seek her for judgment and wise counsel. The Bible never mentions that Deborah's husband had a problem with her being judge over Israel. And it is clear that God confirmed her ministry by the victories experienced by His people under her leadership. Deborah commanded Barak to gather men to engage Sisera in battle. She led and spoke for the fearful Barak, who hesitated to go to Kedesh (on God's command) and meet his opponent Sisera. Barak would not make a move without Deborah. Deborah went with him and spoke the Word of God. Because of her leadership, as Judge and the power of God upon her, many sing her praise; but Deborah had assistance; God-ordained assistance.

It seems that when Barak's opponent (Sisera, general of the army) was in flight, during battle, he fled into the tent of a woman by the name of Jael, the wife of Heber. This woman persuaded Sisera to enter her tent. God has given every woman authority in their position of influence. It is with this influence that Jael ensnared Sisera. This man preferred the woman's tent instead of that of her husband's, because he felt he would be safe there. Yet, in his foolish haste, he did not consider that according to Eastern custom, no man was permitted to intrude into a woman's tent or place of dwelling. To do so meant the death penalty. His entrance, even though it was upon her persuasion, subjected him to the death penalty. He petitioned Jael for something to drink; in her wisdom, Jael gave Sisera milk. He fell asleep in her tent after drinking the milk. Jael was wise enough to adhere to the custom of her day.

God used her to deliver Israel from many years of bitter bondage. While asleep, God used Jael to take a hammer and a tent peg and drive it into Sisera's temple, fastening him into the ground. The battle Barak fought was won because of Deborah's leadership and the wisdom of a woman whose name is rarely mentioned. This is why Deborah told Barak that a woman would get the credit for the victory over Sisera.

Judges 4:4-24

And Deborah, a prophetess, the wife of Lapidoth, she judged Israel at that time. And she dwelt under the palm tree of Deborah between Ramah and Bethel in mount Ephraim: and the children of Israel came up to her for judgment. And she sent and called Barak the son of Abinoam out of Kedeshnaphtali, and said unto him, Hath not the Lord God of Israel commanded, saying, Go and draw toward mount Tabor, and take with thee ten thousand men of the children of Naphtali and of the children of Zebulun? And I will draw unto thee to the river Kishon Sisera, the captain of Jabin's army, with his chariots and his multitude; and I will deliver him into thine hand. And Barak said unto her, If thou wilt go with me, then I will go: but if thou wilt not go with me, then I will not go. And she said, I will surely go with thee: notwithstanding the journey that thou takest shall not be for thine honour; for the Lord shall sell Sisera into the hand of a woman. And Deborah arose, and went with Barak to Kedesh. And Barak called Zebulun and Naphtali to Kedesh; and he went up with ten thousand men at his feet: and Deborah went up with him. Now Heber the

Kenite, which was of the children of Hobab the father in law of Moses, had severed himself from the Kenites, and pitched his tent unto the plain of Zaanaim, which is by Kedesh. And they shewed Sisera that Barak the son of Abinoam was gone up to mount Tabor. And Sisera gathered together all his chariots, even nine hundred chariots of iron, and all the people that were with him, from Harosheth of the Gentiles unto the river of Kishon. And Deborah said unto Barak, Up; for this is the day in which the Lord hath delivered Sisera into thine hand: is not the Lord gone out before thee? So Barak went down from mount Tabor, and ten thousand men after him. And the Lord discomfited Sisera, and all his chariots, and all his host, with the edge of the sword before Barak; so that Sisera lighted down off his chariot, and fled away on his feet. But Barak pursued after the chariots, and after the host, unto Harosheth of the Gentiles: and all the host of Sisera fell upon the edge of the sword; and there was not a man left. Howbeit Sisera fled away on his feet to the tent of Jael the wife of Heber the Kenite: for there was peace between Jabin the king of Hazor and the house of Heber the Kenite. And Jael went out to meet Sisera, and said unto him, Turn in, my lord, turn in to me; fear not. And when he had turned in unto her into the tent, she covered him with a mantle. And he said unto her, Give me, I pray thee, a little water to drink; for I am thirsty. And she opened a bottle of milk, and gave him drink, and covered him. Again he said unto her, Stand in the door of the tent, and it shall be, when any man doth come and inquire of thee, and say, Is there any man here? that thou shalt say, No. Then Jael Heber's wife took a nail of the tent, and took an hammer in her hand, and went softly unto him, and smote the nail into his temples, and fastened it into the ground: for he was fast asleep and weary. So he died. And, behold, as Barak pursued Sisera, Jael came out to meet him, and said unto him, Come, and I will shew thee the man whom thou seekest. And when he came into her tent, behold, Sisera lay dead, and the nail was in his temples. So God subdued on that day Jabin the king of Canaan before the children of Israel. And the hand of the children of Israel prospered, and prevailed against Jabin the king of Canaan, until they had destroyed Jabin king of Canaan.

What a powerful biblical example of God's use of women.

Let's consider a woman by the name of Anna. Anna was a woman from the tribe of Aser and was known as a prophetess. She was at the temple when Simeon spoke joy of having seen the Messiah before his death. In that instant Anna gave thanks also to the Lord and preached of Jesus to all that looked for redemption in Jerusalem. (**Luke 2:38**) In order to prophesy or preach, one must open his or her mouth. Would you agree?

We will clearly see powerful women used of God to fulfill His plan in the earth. We will see that God has no problem with Women in Ministry as Pastors and Teachers, or just members of the Clergy. We will prove so by scripture. Much of the anti-feminist propaganda in the Body of Christ is due to the distortion of Western translators. It is universally known even among the laity that Egypt produced queens as well as Pharaohs. The Candaces of Ethiopia were strong, successful women who were instrumental in charting the destiny of the ancient Christian regions. It is because of the Candace that Ethiopia was one of the first countries to become a Christian nation because she sent her high treasurer, the Ethiopian Eunuch, to Jerusalem to seek information concerning the teaching of Christ.

Acts 8:27
And he arose and went: and, behold, a man of Ethiopia, an eunuch of great authority under Candace queen of the Ethiopians, who had the charge of all her treasure, and had come to Jerusalem for to worship.

There was also a time when Hilkiah and his advisors needed counsel and they went to the prophetess Huldah, who told them comforting words from God.

II Kings 22:14
So Hilkiah the priest, and Ahikam, and Achbor, and Shaphan, and Asahiah, went unto Huldah the prophetess, the wife of Shallum the son of Tikvah, the son of Harhas, keeper of the wardrobe; (now she dwelt in Jerusalem in the college;) and they communed with her.

II Kings 22:15-17
And she said unto them, Thus saith the Lord God of Israel, Tell the man that sent you to me, Thus saith the Lord, Behold, I will bring evil upon this place, and upon the inhabitants thereof, even all the words of the book which the king of Judah hath read: Because they have forsaken me, and have burned incense unto other gods, that they might provoke me to anger with all the works of their hands; therefore my wrath shall be kindled against this place, and shall not be quenched.

In an effort to examine how so much controversy over the roles women may have originated, we must consider the premise used by many to validate their theological stand. It is in the Pauline instructions to Timothy, that many male pastors and religious persons (leaders and laity) have misinterpreted God's plan for woman. For instance, "Let your women keep silent in the church."

I Corinthians 14:34-35

Let your women keep silence in the churches: for it is not permitted unto them to speak; but they are commanded to be under obedience, as also saith the law. And if they will <u>learn</u> anything let them ask their husbands at home: for it is a shame for women to speak in the church.

I Timothy 2:11-15

Let the woman <u>learn</u> in silence with all subjection. But I suffer not a woman to teach, nor to usurp authority over the man, but to be in silence. For Adam was first formed, then Eve. And Adam was not deceived, but the woman being deceived was in the transgression.

Well sure, women should be silent if they are raising as much confusion as the women of Ephesus were doing at that time. Women should be silent if they are uneducated in scriptures and thus spiritual matters (this is explained further in the book). Women being silent have nothing to do with preaching, teaching or prophesying. Paul gave the mentioned statement strictly as an injunction to young Timothy. He was not sending ordinances from God to the early Christian church or the Body of Christ as a whole.

No Biblical scholar can deny that Paul highly accepted women in ministry and on several occasions encouraged other believers to support and assist them. The instructions Paul gave to one local church were not necessarily true for other churches.

During Paul's day, a Rabbi or a teacher could not instruct women in scripture; therefore, women (particularly wives) were ignorant of the scripture. They were told to be silent. They could not teach. If they had questions, they could not disrupt formal service. They were instructed to ask their husbands when they got home (keep reading for further clarity). Paul had to address many sensitive issues in various local churches being established during his day. Needless to say, it was not a commandment from God. There were times when he said, "I speak as a man and not according to the Spirit." Paul's overall objective was not to exclude women from the affairs of God, but to preach the gospel, establish various local churches, and establish order in the church. He would address conflict when a situation warranted his attention. The issue of role distinctions in the Body of Christ, will be debated by some, until the return of the Lord Jesus Christ. The real challenge is whether or not we are willing to allow God open our eyes afresh. A woman who expresses a call to ministry has to give account to God. If God chooses to use a female vessel, what is it to a male or any person for that matter? "For the foolishness of God is wiser than man's wisdom, and the weakness of God is stronger than man's strength."

I Corinthians 1:25-30

Because the foolishness of God is wiser than men; and the weakness of God is stronger than men. For ye see your calling, brethren, how that not many wise men after the flesh, not many mighty, not many noble, are called: But God hath chosen the foolish things of the world to confound the wise; and God hath chosen the weak things of the world to confound the things which are mighty; And base things of the world, and things which are despised, hath God chosen, yea, and things which are not, to bring to nought things that are: That no flesh should glory in his presence. But of him are ye in Christ Jesus, who of God is made unto us wisdom, and righteousness, and sanctification, and redemption...

Genesis 1:26-27

And God said, Let us make <u>man</u> in our image, after our likeness: and <u>let them</u> have dominion over the fish of the sea, and over the fowl of the *air, and over the cattle, and over all the earth, and over every creeping thing that creepeth upon the earth. So God created <u>man</u> in his own image, in the image of God created he him; male and female created he them.*

I would like to emphasize that man; in Genesis 1:26 refers to the species of mankind. Man is "spirit." ___Spirit has no gender___. When it comes to the Ministry of God's Word, gender is not an issue with God and never has been.

Galatians 3:28
There is neither Jew nor Greek, there is neither bond nor free, there is neither male nor female: for ye are all one in Christ Jesus.

I Corinthians 6:17
He that is joined unto the Lord is one spirit.

Man, inclusive of woman, is spirit. In a generic sense, all throughout scripture this is visible. If the following scripture referred to the male-man in gender, what would happen to woman?

II Corinthians 5:17-18
Therefore if any <u>man</u> be in Christ, he is a new creature: old things are passed away; behold, all things are become new. And all things are of God, who hath reconciled us to Himself by Jesus Christ, and hath given to us the ministry of reconciliation;...

"Any man," refers to the species of mankind. The species of mankind is inclusive of male and female. God says all things are of Him and He has given to man and woman the ministry of reconciliation. God is concerned about people. He will use whatever vessel is available to Him to reach the lost, be it male or female. He does not make a distinction between the sexes.

Matthew 16:24
Then said Jesus unto his disciples, if any man (male or female) will come after me, let him deny himself, and take up his cross, and follow me.

John 14:23
Jesus answered and said unto him, if a man (male or female) love me, he will keep my words: and my Father will love him, and we will come unto him, and make our abode with him.

John 13:35
By this shall all men know that ye are my disciples, if ye have love one to another.

Examining all of the above, you would think Jesus only involved the male-man in the things of God if you did not know He was speaking generically. From the beginning, God blessed man and woman and told them to subdue the earth and have dominion over it. These scriptures simply refer to the species of mankind. Mankind differentiates between male and female when it comes to the things of God. However, God does not. God wants His kingdom established in this earth. I will reiterate that He will work through whatever vessel is yielded and available to Him regardless of gender. God does not confirm gender; He confirms His Word.

Mark 16:17-20
And these signs shall follow them that believe; in my name shall they cast out devils; they shall speak with new tongues; they shall take up serpents; and if they drink any deadly thing, it shall not hurt them; they shall lay hands on the sick, and they shall recover. So then after the Lord had spoken unto them, he was received up into heaven, and sat on the right hand of God. And they went forth, and preached every where,

the Lord working with them, and confirming the word with signs following. Amen.

God says these signs will follow those who believe, not those who are of the male sex. There are no superior or inferior believers in the eyes of God. The male-man is not more spiritual than the female-man. We are all the sons and daughters of God with the authority of God, empowered to operate like God. We have joint-heirship with Jesus.

I John 3:1-2
Behold, what manner of love the Father hath bestowed upon us, that we should be called the sons of God: therefore the world knoweth us not, because it knew him not. Beloved, now are we the sons of God, and it doth not yet appear what we shall be: but we know that, when he shall appear, we shall be like him; for we shall see him as he is.

Romans 8:14-15
For as many as are led by the Spirit of God, they are the sons of God. For ye have not received the spirit of bondage again to fear; but ye have received the Spirit of adoption, whereby we cry, Abba, Father. The Spirit himself bears witness with our spirit, that we are the children of God.

I Peter 2:9
But ye are a chosen generation, a royal priesthood, an holy nation, a peculiar people: that ye should shew forth the praises of him who hath called you out of darkness into his marvelous light.

Without proper interpretation of scripture, some would conclude that God totally excluded women from the mentioned scriptures. Thank God we can clearly discern the truth. Whether the term used says sons, brethren, man, he or him, the Bible is written for the children of God, and we know God included woman in His plan to minister life to the lost through His Word. With this in mind, there is a powerful story in **Numbers, Chapter 22**, from which we can learn some awesome truths. Consider the following:

God caused the children of Israel to be extremely victorious over their enemies. In **Numbers 22:1-35,** Israel is camped in the plains of Moab. Because of their victory over Sihon, King of the Amorites and Og, King of Bashan, Balak, King of Moab, all of Moab was afraid of Israel. The Israelites were God's chosen people and God was with them as long as they obeyed his commands. Balak heard of the prophet Balaam and sent great riches and messengers to persuade Balaam to come and curse this mighty company of people. Balak felt that if Balaam cursed the Israelites, he and all Moab could prevail against them and drive them from the plains of Moab. Balaam sought the face of God and God instructed Balaam to not go with the elders of Moab and the elders of Midian. God told Balaam that the children of Israel were blessed. Balaam told the elders of Moab and the elders of Midian what God told him and sent them on their way. Yet, Balak was persistent. He sent greater wealth to Balaam a second time and promised to greatly promote him. Balaam answered by telling Balak's messengers that no matter what he offered him, he could not go beyond the Word of God for any amount of reward. There is a point that should be evaluated carefully, because Balaam's mouth spoke one thing, but his heart another. Balaam did not send Balak's messengers away. Instead, this time, he persuaded them to spend the night. Even though God made his instructions explicitly clear to Balaam the first time, Balaam went back to God a second time and petitioned Him concerning going with the messengers of Balak, as if God had changed his mind overnight. Balaam was interested in the rewards.

The pull of man's flesh, and the corruption in his heart will always cause him to waver in his commitment to holiness and doubt the express will of God if he does not know how to resist temptation and obey God's instructions to the letter. Because of the persistence of Balaam and the greed in his heart, God was angered and gave him leave to go to Moab even though this was not His perfect will. While riding on his ass, the Angel of the Lord was standing in the way with His sword drawn in His hand to kill Balaam. However, Balaam could not see the Angel of the Lord. His ass saw the angel and in an effort to save Balaam's life turned aside out of the way and went into the field. As a result, Balaam smote the ass.

Again, Balaam headed towards Moab, and again, the ass, seeing the angel, thrust herself into the wall and crushed Balaam's foot against the wall. Balaam, once again, smote the ass. Balaam is so blinded by greed and his own selfish interest; he did not see that his life was in danger. The angel of the Lord stood in a narrow place where there was no way to turn, either to the right hand or to the left. When the ass saw the Angel of the Lord, she fell down under Balaam. Balaam's anger was kindled, and he smote the ass with a staff and the Lord opened the mouth of the ass, and she said unto Balaam, "What have I done unto thee, that thou hast smitten me these three times?" And Balaam said unto the ass, "Because thou hast mocked me. I would there was a sword in mine hand for now would I kill thee." And the ass said unto Balaam, "Am not I thine ass, upon which thou hast ridden ever since I was thine unto this day? Was I ever wont to do so unto thee?" And he said, "Nay." Then the Lord opened the eyes of Balaam, and he saw the Angel of the Lord standing in the way and His sword drawn in his hand and he bowed down his head, and fell flat on his face and the angel of the Lord said unto him, "Wherefore hast thou smitten thine ass these three times? Behold, I was out to withstand thee because thy way is perverse before me, and the ass saw me and turned from me these three times. Unless the ass had turned from me, surely now also I had slain thee, and saved her alive."

Now look at what is happening here! The first point I would like to make is that an "ass" is a female donkey. The second point is that animals do not have a spirit. They are not tripartite in being, as man. They have no need of an atoning sacrifice. There is no redemption for them. God does something supernatural. He opens the eyes of an ass and causes her to see into the realm of the spirit. She attempts to protect her master's life, but Balaam, blinded by what he wanted to do, as many are today, could not see that he was headed for destruction.

Many, today, are blinded by philosophies, religious traditions, oppressive theological persuasions, greed, pride, egotistical strongholds, denominational bondages, and the "spirit of error." They cannot see they are on a course that leads to destruction.

Balaam was so caught up in what he wanted to do, until, he did not realize he was talking to an ass. An ass was an animal that was known to be stubborn. He was so engulfed in his pursuit, until he did not realize that the ass was questioning his actions. Instead, he begins explaining his actions to the ass. Whenever we are blinded by our own ambitions, our own greed, our own lust, our own pride, we will find ourselves destined for spiritual decline.

Proverbs 14:12
There is a way which seemeth right unto a man,
but the end thereof are the ways of death.

God uses a female ass to declare truth to persuade Balaam of the error of his ways. While Balaam was in conversation with his ass, God opens Balaam's eyes. It is then that Balaam realizes the error of his ways. Man is unable to see the devastation of his ways without God.

If God will use a female ass to proclaim truth, who is man to say that God will not use women to preach, teach, or pastor? Men can be blinded to truth and it takes the power of God to open their eyes so that they can see. Balaam saw that the ass was trying to protect him from destruction when God opened his eyes. When he saw the Angel of the Lord, he fell flat on his face. The sword was drawn and the Angel of the Lord explained to

Balaam that he was as good as dead if it had not been for his ass. Many men in leadership refuse to accept women in ministry. The emphasis should not be on whom God uses, but that God's plan and purpose for all men be fulfilled.

God is not a God of traditions. He has no respect of gender or denominations. He is Spirit and He is Truth. Any woman proclaiming the truth of God cannot be an enemy to God, but she is an awesome terror to the forces of darkness. God will use the weak things of this world to confound the wise.

I Corinthians 1:26-29

For ye see your calling, brethren, how that not many wise men after the flesh, not many mighty, not many noble, are called: But God hath chosen the foolish things of the world to confound the wise; and God hath chosen the weak things of the world to confound the things which are mighty; and the base things of the world, and things which are despised, hath God chosen, yea, and things which are not to bring to nought things that are: that no flesh should glory in his presence.

Acts 2:17

And it shall come to pass in the last days, saith God, I will pour out of my Spirit upon all flesh: and your sons and your daughters shall prophesy, and your young men shall see visions, and your old men shall dream dreams: and on my servants and on my handmaidens I will pour out in those days of my Spirit; and they shall prophesy.

God includes the male-man and the female-man in the above scriptures. He promised that He would pour out His Spirit upon sons and daughters and they would prophesy. Prophecy is for the church and it is in order to prophesy in a general assembly as long as one is submitted to the authority of the Pastor and respectful of the order of the church. To prophesy means to speak to men (male and female) to edification, exhortation and comfort. In the Corinthian church, there were many problems. Many say, **I Corinthians 14:34-35** proves that God does not use women to preach; however, in this scripture Paul was not speaking of teaching or preaching. He was responding to women who were bringing about disturbance in the public worship services. The disturbance and confusion had nothing to do with teaching and preaching. The custom during the time of the Corinthian church was that men could speak up in public assemblies to ask questions and even interrupt the speaker when they did not understand. This liberty was not granted to the women. The word "women," in this passage, refers to wives and as you will see in a later chapter, there is no word in the Greek that distinguishes woman from wife in the King James Version. Therefore, the context must reveal whether Paul was addressing married women, unmarried women or women in general.

Wives were considered their husband's property. Many would blurt out in the public worship services and disrupt the service. Rather than keep confusion going in the church, they were told to be quiet in public worship, and if they had a question or did not understand something, instead of blurting out, they were to ask their husbands at home. Wives were admonished to ask questions at home so as not to disrupt the worship services or bring embarrassment upon their husbands. However, women could pray and prophesy in the general assembly. All things had to be done decently and in order. We must also realize that grace and truth came by Jesus Christ. **(John 1:17)** Women are not bound to the law any longer. We are saved by grace through our faith (**Ephesians 2:8**) in the redemptive work of Christ.

I Corinthians 14:34-35

Let your women (wives) keep silence in the churches: for it is not permitted unto them to speak; but they are commanded to be under obedience, as also saith the law. And if they will learn anything let them ask their husbands at home: for it is a shame for women (wives) to speak in the church.

Now let's consider several factors from Paul's letter to Timothy. He tells the women to learn in silence. This has nothing to do with her preaching or pastoring. Then Paul says the woman is not allowed to speak. Well, who initiated this rule? Was it God or man? Under the law, women would be stoned if they did not obey their husbands. Paul says, "It is a shame for women (wives) to speak in church." He is referring to women (wives) blurting out in an assembly, with little or no knowledge of what they were saying, starting confusion, embarrassing their husbands, and interrupting the speakers. During this time women were not instructed in the scripture as men. Paul addresses the issue of women usurping authority over the man by not respecting the position of authority God gave man. Paul reminds Timothy that God made woman for man to assist him in all God called him to be. Adam was formed first, but God said it was not good for Adam to be alone and fashioned someone suitable and adaptable to Adam, a help-meet. Women usurp authority over men when they disrespect his God-ordained position, not when they preach the gospel. While preaching the gospel, every woman must be under the authority of a Godly man.

I Timothy 2:11-15

Let the woman learn in silence with all subjection. But I suffer not a woman to teach, nor to usurp authority over the man, but to be in silence. For Adam was first formed, then Eve. And Adam was not deceived, but the woman being deceived was in the transgression.

Women represent the female aspect of the God-Head. Women are more emotional than men. God designed the woman to be a life-giver. Women are responders. But women are also created in the image and likeness of God. **(Genesis 1:26)** Because of a woman's make-up, women are more readily deceived (as was the case with Eve) than men. Therefore, in an effort to protect us, God gave the male man authority over the female man to protect her. God gave woman the power of influence. Paul could not have been telling women not to teach or preach because look at what he tells Titus in the following scripture:

Titus 2:1-5

But speak thou the things which become sound doctrine: That the aged men be sober, grave, temperate, sound in faith, in charity, in patience. The aged <u>women likewise</u>, that they be in behavior as becometh holiness, not false accusers, not given to much wine, <u>teachers of good things; That they may teach the young women to be sober, to love their husbands, to love their children, to be discreet, chaste, keepers at home, good, obedient to their own husbands, that the word of God be not blasphemed</u>.

Acts 21:8-9

And the next day we that were of Paul's company departed, and came unto Caesarea: and we entered into the house of Philip the evangelist, which was one of the seven; and abode with him. <u>And the same man had four daughters, virgins, which did prophesy</u>.

The first word Jesus sent to His disciples advising them that He was risen from the dead was sent by a female.

John 20:11-17

But Mary stood without at the sepulchre weeping: and as she wept, she stooped down, and looked into the sepulchre, And seeth two angels in white sitting, the one at the head, and the other at the feet, where the body of Jesus had lain. And they say unto her, Woman, why weepest thou? She saith unto them, because they have taken away my Lord, and I know not where they have laid him. And when she had thus said, she turned herself back, and saw Jesus standing, and knew not that it was Jesus. Jesus saith unto her, Woman, why weepest thou? Whom seekest thou? She, supposing him to be the gardener, saith unto him, Sir, if thou have borne him hence, tell me where thou hast laid him, and I will take him away. Jesus saith unto her, Mary. She turned herself, and saith unto him, Rabboni; which is to say, Master. Jesus saith unto her, touch me not; for I am not yet ascended to my Father: but go to my brethren, and say unto them, I ascend unto my Father, and your Father; and to my God, and your God.

The Samaritan woman evangelized an entire city after her encounter with the Messiah. Paul advised various churches to support the women who had labored with him in the gospel. Women were the last at the cross and first at the tomb. Yes, God does use women as Ministers, Pastors and Teachers. He is the same yesterday and today and forever. **(Hebrews 13:8)** He changes not and He is no respector of persons.

Malachi 3:6
For I am the Lord, I change not; therefore ye sons of Jacob are not consumed.

Romans 16:1-2
I commend unto you <u>Phebe</u> our sister, which is <u>a servant of the church which is at Cenchrea</u>; that ye receive her in the Lord, as becometh saints, and that ye assist her in whatsoever business she hath need of you; for she hath been a succourer of many, and of myself also.

Romans 16:3-4

Greet Priscilla and Aquila my helpers in Christ Jesus: who have for my life laid down their own necks: unto whom not only I give thanks, but also all the churches of the Gentiles.

In the above scriptures Paul speaks highly of **Phebe**, a female Pastor. Then he speaks highly of a husband and wife team, Priscilla and her husband Aquila. Contrary to the usual custom of the day, Paul acknowledges the wife Priscilla and then her husband Aquila. Even though he did not come to enjoy the rich rewards of a marital relationship by choice, Paul esteemed women highly. He supported them in ministry and encouraged others to support them.

Chapter Two

God's Order for the Family

In order for any corporation, business, organization or entity to be successful, there must be structure. There must be organization. There must be rules; and there must be regulations. A chain of command must exist and there must be those who respect and adhere to the rules, regulations, and chain of command. No entity can function successfully and remain strong without the above elements. Marriage and the order established in the family unit is ordained by God. Because God loves us, and has always endeavored to provide the best for us, He knew that in order for a marriage or family unit to receive maximum fulfillment and enjoy ultimate success, there must be order. God did not take Adam and Eve and thrust them into a chaotic situation after forming them. He first established order in the earth, prepared a place for them to live, created them and gave them instructions.

Genesis 2:8
And the Lord God planted a garden eastward in Eden: and there he put the man whom he had formed.

God's will for us has always been that we live our lives free from chaos and disharmony. He is the one who initiates structure and order in the family. The reason is clear. Where God's mandates are priority, every family member can enjoy maximum fulfillment, success, and security. He ordained the union of marriage to protect the man, the woman and the children. To operate by God's order brings lasting peace and reward. **Marriage** is a divine institution created by God, whereby, two imperfect, rational, free moral agents, of the opposite sex, who are born again, choose to enter into covenant relationship with each other, forsaking all others, and have made an unconditional, lifetime commitment to God to live with an imperfect person until death.

Before we examine God's order for the family, I want to establish a foundation by which we clearly see God's divine plan for every believer and how this plan contributes to the flow of God's order for the family. When every member of the Body of Christ understands God's order for the family and functions therein, our churches will be stronger in commitment, and our testimony in the earth as the people of God will encourage thousands to receive Jesus as Lord and Savior. This truth is so important because whatever is in the home infiltrates the church. If we have strong families, respecting the order of God domestically (naturally), we will have strong churches with members respecting the order of God spiritually.

Ephesians 5:1-2
Be ye therefore followers of God, as dear children; and walk in love, as Christ also hath loved us, and hath given himself for us an offering and a sacrifice to God for a sweet smelling savour.

In order to understand the ways of God, and function as He requires in all areas of life, we must first learn how to be followers of God in everything. We must adhere to His mandates for life in the home, in the Body of Christ, and as we observe the civil laws of the land.

The word "follower" in **Ephesians 5:1**, comes from the Greek word "**mimetes**," which means to mimic (imitate) the speech, behavior, or ways of God. God instructs us to imitate "HIM", as children imitate their parents. Then, He says, walk, in love, as Christ also hath loved you. God is instructing us to possess a lifestyle that is governed by love and unselfish behavior. He encourages us to walk in love one with another even as Christ loved us enough to voluntarily lay down His life as a sacrifice for all humanity. Jesus loves us so much that He made it possible for all men to experience redemption by His blood.

John 3:16-17
For God so loved the world, that He gave His only begotten Son, that whosoever believeth in Him should not perish, but have everlasting life. For God sent not His Son into the world to condemn the world; but that the world through Him might be saved.

Redemption comes from the Greek word "APOLUTROSIS," which reveals man's liberation from the guilt and the doom of sin. Redemption is the introduction into a life of liberty, "newness of life". God requires that we love each other so much that we are willing to give up our lives so that others may live. To give up one's life does not necessarily refer to physical death, but it is the ability to deny one's self in order that another may be blessed; others may be brought to the highest possible level of growth and development. It is the ability to esteem others better than ourselves. This is what Jesus did. **(Philippians 2:5-11)** He looked at the deplorable state of man and humbled himself in obedience to God and submitted Himself to death for the sake of all mankind. I must say that we have not matured in love to this degree.

If we imitate God in all manner of living, we will not engage in sex outside of the confines of marriage. We will abstain from all uncleanness in any form and we will always govern the words that fall from our lips. This type of lifestyle emanates from one who truly imitates God. God tells us precisely why we must refrain from foolish talking, fornication, uncleanness, covetousness, and so much more. As we follow the next several verses in Ephesians, we understand the essence of what is said.

Ephesians 5:3-4
But fornication, and all uncleanness, or covetousness, let it not be once named among you,

25

*as becometh saints; neither filthiness, nor foolish
talking, nor jesting which are not convenient, but
rather giving thanks.*

Ephesians 5:5-7
*For this ye know, that no whoremonger, nor
unclean person, nor covetous man, who is an
idolater, hath any inheritance in the kingdom of
Christ and of God. Let no man deceive you with
vain words: for because of these things cometh the
wrath of God upon the children of disobedience.
Be not ye therefore partakers with them.*

God's divine order for His children is initiated to protect
our lives. We must daily adhere to God's Word if we intend to
enjoy the full benefits of being children of God, enjoy a good
life, wholesome relationships, fulfillment and peace. These are
all benefits of being in the kingdom of God.

It is encumbered upon us to govern our lives by the Word of
God without deviation. God tells us that there was a time when
we walked in darkness. There was a time when we had no concept
of spiritual truth, no awareness of spiritual principles or realities.
There was a time when we had no awareness of the ways and
plans of God, but that time is past. God has given us illumination,
insight, and a keener intelligence of who He is and how He wants
us to live on this earth and He fully expects us to comply with His
plan and purpose for our lives.

Ephesians 5:8-15
*For ye were sometimes darkness, but now are
ye light in the Lord: walk as children of light:
for the fruit of the Spirit is in all goodness
and righteousness and truth; proving what is
acceptable unto the Lord. And have no fellowship
with the unfruitful works of darkness, but rather
reprove them. For it is a shame even to speak of
those things which are done of them in secret. But*

all things that are reproved are made manifest by the light: for whatsoever doth make manifest is light. Wherefore he saith, awake thou that sleepest, and arise from the dead and Christ shall give thee light. See then that ye walk circumspectly (carefully considering all circumstances and possible consequences), not as fools, but as wise.

The Word of God distinctively reveals that darkness cannot stand up against light. It is utterly exposed and dispelled when it confronts truth. All lies will be exposed. Truth is unchanging and can be verified. Truth depicts holiness and the essence of who Christ is. We are admonished, as believers, to awake by the awesome power of God's presence. He encourages us to turn away from wickedness and look to Him who gives spiritual awareness and life forevermore. As the people of God, we must hate evil and observe at all times our conduct and manner of living. We must be on our guard, standing firm against those who would attempt to distract us. God has chosen us to represent Him in this earth and be a visible demonstration of His power to those who walk in darkness. Light refers to understanding or illumination of spiritual truth as a result of one being born into the family of God.

Ephesians 5:16-20

Redeeming the time because the days are evil. Wherefore, be ye not unwise, but understanding what the will of the Lord is. And be not drunk with wine, wherein is excess; but be filled with the Spirit; speaking to yourselves in psalms and hymns and spiritual songs, singing and making melody in your hearts to the Lord; giving thanks always for all things unto God and the Father in the name of our Lord Jesus Christ.

After considering verses **Ephesians 5:1-20**, the total essence of what Paul is saying to the church at Ephesus is that we have no time to waste on petty differences. We must not be ignorant concerning God's will. We have no time to be anesthetized by artificial stimuli, or bogged down with religious or doctrinal differences. God has instructed us to be watchful and serious minded. He calls us to be filled with the Holy Spirit. Why? Because the Holy Spirit brings organization into the believer's life and enables us to respond correctly to the Word of God. He sanctifies the believer for the work of the ministry and anoints the believer with power, which enables us to resist sin. He directs the believer and He gives us the boldness to stand in the face of what seems to be defeat and declare victory over the forces of evil and the pull of the flesh.

Now we reach the heart of the 5th chapter of Ephesians. The preceding verses encourage every believer to examine himself, and eliminate all ungodliness. Paul sets all things in order by instructing believers to achieve a great accomplishment, "***Submit yourselves to one another***." It takes a believer, who really knows who they are in Christ, to commit to a walk of humility and submit to other believers in the Body of Christ. For far too long "submission" has been depicted as something degrading and negative. However, God ordained it to be a delightful experience. It has the awesome power to persuade, to win over. When believers submit one to another, it gives evidence that we have confidence first in God, secondly we have confidence in the Spirit of God in other members of the Body of Christ and therefore, we are freely able to esteem others better than ourselves. Because of our love and respect for God's divine order, we willingly choose to submit to one another.

Ephesians 5:21
Submitting yourselves one to another in the fear of the Lord.

When we acknowledge God, we have reverential respect for who He is; His indwelling presence in other members of the Body. What He has commissioned us to do compels us to recognize the gift of God in every believer. With respect for the gift, we understand that God has given every believer something uniquely different to bless and enhance the Body of Christ. Therefore, in order to submit to one another we must first learn submission to God and to His order and respect the gift of God in every member of the Body. This is why I prefaced this chapter with **Ephesians 5:1-21**. We must first respect God by imitating Him. We must literally conform to His character, speech, and likeness in all arenas of life. We must alienate ourselves from anything and anyone who will contaminate the manner of living we have chosen by our respect and love for God. When I submit to God, I am saying God's way is perfect. His way is flawless and I choose to govern my life by a higher order. I choose to obey one who has my best interest at heart and His plan is designed to protect my life. Therefore, I freely yield and accept His way as the best way.

Now we are ready for verse 22. It is in this verse that God leads us into His divine order for the family. In these verses, Paul takes the occasion to show how the husband-wife relationship illustrates the relationship of Christ to His Church. Paul encourages husbands to love their wives as Christ loves the church and He encourages wives to submit to their own husbands. How did Christ love the church? (1) He was an example to the church; (2) He was servant to the church; (3) He deprived Himself for the sake of the church; so must every husband be to his wife. Every husband must be a Godly example. Every husband must serve his family. Every husband must deprive himself, if need be, for the sake of his wife and his children.

Ephesians 5:22
Wives, submit yourselves unto your own husbands as unto the Lord.

The Greek word for "***submit***" is "hupotasso". Translated into English it means to subject. The Greek word used for "man" and for "husband" in the New Testament is the same word, "aner." The Greek of the New Testament had no separate word for "husband;" neither did it have a separate word to distinguish "woman" from "wife." The Greek word for woman is "gyne". Therefore, the Greek word for "woman" is the same for "wife." It must be determined by the context which of these meanings should be given to the words in the English passage. We can determine from the context in which Paul is speaking whether he is talking about women in general, or strictly about wives. There are times when Paul talks about women in general, but at other times he is explicitly talking about wives.

Each passage must be properly interpreted by the inspiration of the Holy Spirit and in light of all scripture references on the topic. In **Ephesians 5:22**, notice that God, through the Apostle Paul, does not tell single women to submit to every man, nor does He tell the married woman to submit to every woman's husband. God explicitly addresses the married woman and He tells her to submit to her own husband, not Sally's husband, but her own husband. This is clearly speaking within the confines of marriage.

In the Body of Christ, He says, believers submit yourselves to one another. This means men submit to women and women submit to men in the Body of Christ. Clearly a man can submit to the pastoral leadership of a female; even as a female submits to the pastoral leadership of a male. The key here is to recognize that in the Body of Christ, the gender of leadership is not the issue, but the ability of all members in the Body to respect the presence of God in one another. Remember, our submission must be as unto the Lord. No believer should attempt to fight or do anything unseemly to achieve his own way, but every believer should yield one to another as to the Lord for order's sake.

However, in the family unit, God instructs the wife to submit to the husband. Submission must be an act of a woman's own free will to yield to the one man who has vowed before God to protect her, love her and cherish her forever. The husband teaches his wife submission by his submission first and foremost to Almighty God. His visible demonstration of the Lordship of Jesus Christ in His life, commands the respect of the wife; and because she sees the power in the husband's obedience to God, she willingly gives up her way to submit to him as unto the Lord.

Ephesians 5:23-24

For the husband is the head of the wife, even as Christ is the head of the church: and he is the saviour of the body. Therefore as the church is subject unto Christ, so let the wives be to their own husbands in every thing.

God likens the relationship that a husband and wife enjoy domestically to the spiritual relationship Jesus has to the church. The above scripture reveals that the husband influences the wife, even as Christ influences every member of the Body of Christ and as Christ is the Saviour of the Body of Christ, the husband is the saviour of his family. The word "saviour," as it relates to the husband, refers to his obligation to protect his wife from danger and destruction. The Apostle Paul states that even as believers submit to Christ, wives subject themselves to their own husbands in everything. Now let me qualify, **<u>in everything</u>**" by stating that this refers to everything that is pleasing in the eyes of the Lord. The husband walks in moral excellence and requires that of his wife as well. A wife is under no obligation to violate the commandments of God to please her husband.

The husband is not Christ; neither is he his wife's spiritual authority. He is just what the Bible says. He is the husband and in the natural order of the family God has commissioned the husband to fulfill the role of leader in the home. **He is her natural example before God, not her spiritual head**. When the scripture says he is the head of the wife, it simply means he is to guide his wife, as it is pleasing to the Lord. He is summoned by God to love his wife and to protect her even as Christ is the spiritual head of the Church. He gives the church protection. He sustains the church by His Word. He redeemed us with His blood. He gives us direction and guidance and He ever liveth to make intercession for us. The word "Head" simply refers to one who influences or gives direction to.

Hebrews 7:25

Wherefore he is able also to save them to the uttermost that come unto God by him, seeing he ever liveth to make intercession for them.

Therefore, the husband should pray for His wife, direct his wife by Godly influence, protect his wife, and provide for his wife.

Submission to the husband, in all things, is based upon the husband loving the wife as Christ loves the church. When a wife knows that her husband always has her best interest at heart, and that her total fulfillment in life is of paramount importance to him, she does not mind yielding to his leadership. No woman is required to submit to verbal, mental, or physical abuse. A woman is not under obligation to submit to a husband's cruelty or perverted desires.

The Bible distinctively reveals the love Christ has for the Church. If a man truly loves his wife, the way Jesus loves the church, his submission to God will generate an atmosphere in the home that is conducive to submission on behalf of the wife and the children. Why? Because the family has a visible demonstration of the obedience of the husband (father) to God and the rewards of his outward obedience. Therefore, this demonstration releases the other members of the family to order their behavior by what is seen. We cannot be, what we cannot see.

Ephesians 5:25-33

Husbands love your wives, even as Christ also loved the Church, and gave Himself for it; that He might sanctify and cleanse it with the washing of water by the Word. That he might present it to Himself a glorious church not having spot or wrinkle, or any such thing; but that it should be holy and without blemish. So ought men to love their wives as their own bodies. He that loveth his wife loveth himself. For no man ever yet hated his own flesh; but nourisheth and cherisheth it, even as the Lord the church: for we are members of his body, of his flesh, and of his bones. For this cause shall a man leave his father and mother and shall be joined unto his wife and they two shall be one flesh. This is a great mystery: but I speak concerning Christ and the Church. Nevertheless let every one of you in particular so love his wife even as himself: and the wife sees that she reverence her husband.

It is not difficult to see that God inspired Paul to draw a comparison between the relationship of Christ to the Church and the relationship of a husband to his wife. There can be no dispute as to the love of Christ for His Bride (the Church). Therefore, the family must model this relationship. God has given us a visible demonstration of how He wants the family structured and how every member is accountable. No man can mistreat his wife justifiably before God and no woman can justifiably deny that God placed the husband over her, to pray for her, to provide for her and to protect her from danger.

A very simple, natural illustration comes from a law that was passed requiring every person driving an automobile to wear a seat-belt. The purpose of a seat-belt is to restrain a person in the event of collision, in an effort to sustain life. It was designed to restrict, for protection. The law states that it is illegal to drive an automobile without the seat-belt being intact. The driver may be an extremely cautious driver with an excellent driving history. The driver's ability is not in question. He is simply admonished to submit to the law for his protection. The seat-belt may be uncomfortable initially, but becomes a way of life as a result of respect for the authorities, consistent obedience and because the purpose has been defined. In the event of a collision, the driver is held in place so as not to be thrown from the automobile and killed.

In the marital relationship the husband is much like a seat-belt to his wife and children. He serves as an instrument to hold the family safely intact, until Jesus returns for His bride. He does not desire to restrict any member of the family, but must set guidelines in place so that every member reaches full potential. Life initially may be uncomfortable, but when the purpose of the guidelines is explained, every member can adhere to those guidelines and function therein in absolute harmony, unity and order. The husband nourishes his wife and children as his own body. The word "nourish" means to cherish, care for and protect. It comes from the Greek word "thalpo" which means to foster the growth of.

I Peter 3:7

Likewise, ye husbands, dwell with them according
to knowledge, giving honour unto the wife, as unto
the weaker vessel, and as being heirs together of
the grace of life; that your prayers be not hindered.

Husbands are instructed to dwell with their wives according to knowledge. Where does this knowledge come from? It comes from the man developing his relationship with God, through fellowship with God and study of the scriptures. God ordained that the husband's relationship with his "Maker" overflow into his relationship with his wife. The husband honors his wife as the physically weaker, because women are more emotional than men and the design of a woman's body was not built, in strength, to equal a man. The emphasis is not on who is the stronger physically or spiritually, but that both are heirs together of the grace of life. Both are children of God and should be respected by one another as a son and a daughter of God with the same rights and privileges.

To violate God's instructions causes their prayer life to be virtually ineffective.

The wife of a husband who follows God's instructions experiences her husband's own submission to her, and thereby, each partner shares in the blessed state of surrender one to another as unto Christ. This is why women must be extremely wise concerning whom they marry. A man who is not submitted to God does not know how to submit to his wife and cannot love her as Christ loves the Church. If he is not saved, he is a child of the devil, with the nature of the devil, and will therefore, be influenced by the kingdom of darkness. He has not experienced the love of God; therefore, he does not know the true essence of love. He cannot love himself or anyone else, until he has first experienced the love of God.

Many people have abused the word submission by equating it with a derogatory connotation. On the contrary, there is power in submission and it takes spiritually mature believers to understand the strength therein. For the sake of order and structure, domestically, the husband should be the head of the house. He is given the position of authority and the woman is given the position of influence. A man who knows who he is in Christ and who is knowledgeable of his rights and privileges in the family of God, can keep demons from disrupting his home and deceiving his wife. A truth that many women are ignorant of is that women are more easily deceived than men because we are more emotional than men. Every woman needs Godly protection from a man of God; whether that man is father, grandfather, uncle, cousin, brother, or husband.

Women are also extremely sensitive to the leading of the Holy Spirit and will give our all to the Lord. We will launch out hastily into ministry, because we are life-givers; we are responders. We long to respond to the call of God and give birth to the plans and purposes of God. However, our haste could lead to some very devastating experiences if not regulated by a Godly man. God is more concerned about us fulfilling the call than we are, and He will use our husbands to lead us in the way of wisdom. Satan loves to see women launch into ministry prematurely. For this reason, God placed the male-man over the female-man for the purpose of protecting her from demonic influence and manipulation. This is why God told Eve her desire would be to her husband.

Genesis 3:16

Unto the woman he said, I will greatly multiply thy sorrow and thy conception; in sorrow thou shall bring forth, children; and thy desire shall be to thy husband, and he shall rule over thee.

God has given every woman a desire to respond to the male influence in her life. Women desire Godly male leadership. Women desire to respond. This is why many are on an all out search for a husband, and many fall into pre-marital sexual relationships. This is the end-result when women operate outside of God's divine order. God never ordained that women seek out a husband or male companionship. Compromise leads to destruction.

Proverbs 18:22

Whoso findeth a wife findeth a good thing, and obtaineth favor of the Lord.

Proverbs 31:10

Who can find a virtuous woman? For her price is far above rubies.

Since women are responders and desire Godly male leadership, we can certainly understand why it is imperative that the male influence in a woman's life be totally surrendered to God.

The word "**rule**" in **Genesis 3:16** means to guide, or regulate by an established standard or influence. When God formed Adam and made woman, He gave them equal dominion. Adam had authority and so did Eve. There was no regulator for woman. She had and still has authority in the realm of influence. However, when she was deceived and caused Adam to rebel against God, God placed man over her as a regulator to direct the authority He had given her; to direct her power. Women are powerful instruments in the hands of God and powerful, vessels in the arena of influence. We can clearly see this in the lives of Eve, Ruth, Esther, Jeezebel, Delilah, Sarah, and Mary, the mother of

Jesus. The power God has invested in the female must be shielded or regulated; therefore, God gave the male-man authority over woman to assist in directing the power within. A female Pastor should be married. She must be submitted to the authority of her husband so she can receive counsel or direction, when necessary.

Genesis 1:26-28

And God said, Let us make man (species of mankind-male and female) in our image, and after our likeness: and let them have dominion over the fish of the sea, and over the fowl of the air, and over the cattle, and over all the earth, and over every creeping thing that creepeth upon the earth. So God created man in his own image, in the image of God created he him; male and female created he them. And God blessed them, and God said unto them, be fruitful, and multiply, and replenish the earth, and subdue it: and have dominion over the fish of the sea, and over the fowl of the air and over every living thing that creepeth upon the earth.

The above scripture clearly reveals that God made man and woman to have joint rulership and dominion over the earth. I believe a woman has always desired to please her husband, but, after the fall, God placed in woman a deeper yearning to respond to or please her husband in order that she draw closer to him as the authority set in place to bring her to full spiritual maturity and development, free from any interruption by the forces of darkness. In a later chapter we will discuss the fact that a born-again woman is no longer subject to the curse of the law, any more than a born again man is.

The enemy seeks to destroy women by a powerful element used on Eve, "deception." The word "deceive" comes from the Greek word, "exapatao" which means to beguile thoroughly, or deceive wholly.

I Timothy 2:14

And Adam was not deceived, but the woman being deceived was in the transgression.

The **spiritual** "head" of male and female, married or unmarried is Christ. When a woman has the call of God upon her life, it is important that **she minister under authority**. When anyone ministers outside of authority, satan enters in and influences that person to function by an evil spirit. Flaky, invalid revelations will come to those who operate in rebellion or who are not operating under proper authority. Within authority there is a hedge of protection. Outside authority is a vacuum of defeat.

I Corinthians 11:1-5

Be ye followers of me, even as I also am of Christ. Now I praise you, brethren, that ye remember me in all things, and keep the ordinances, as I delivered them to you. But I would have you know, that the head of every man is Christ; and the head of the woman is the man; and the head of Christ is God. Every man praying or prophesying, having his head covered, dishonoureth his head. But every woman that prayeth or prophesieth with her head uncovered dishonoureth her head: for that is even all one as if she were shaven.

Paul is dealing with divine order in the above verses. Spiritually, he is dealing with the absence of authority. A man or a woman who prophesied with an uncovered head (outside of authority) was functioning out of order. To function out of order is to function outside of the authority that God has ordained to be over his people. If we function outside of authority, we dishonor our head, who is Christ. God has established perimeters within the home and perimeters within the church. When we step outside of the order of God, we leave God's divine order, becoming open prey for the enemy.

The Apostle Paul received reports from Christians in many of the churches concerning problems believers encountered. He responded to their questions and concerns regarding life, conduct, doctrinal differences, and so much more. Let me emphasize that there must be order (structure) established in the home. God gives wives a command to submit to the Godly leadership of their husbands. He tells the husbands to love their wives and do not provoke them to be bitter. Then God tells the children to obey your parents. God inspired the Apostle to outline His order for the family. Can you imagine what it would be like to have children telling the father what to do, and the mother obeying the children? What a chaotic situation in light of the child's inexperience, lack of knowledge and immaturity. It is sad to say that many parents are allowing their children to violate God's order, because they refuse to discipline their children. The following scriptures reveal God's mind on the issue of discipline.

Ephesians 6:1-4
Children, obey your parents in the Lord: for this is right. Honour thy father and mother; which is the first commandment with promise: that it may be well with thee, and thou mayst live long on the earth. And ye fathers, provoke not your children to wrath: but bring them up in the nurture and admonition of the Lord.

Proverbs 22:6
Train up a child in the way he should go: and when he is old, he will not depart from it.

The above scriptures simply mean parents must train or hedge in a child in the way he or she should go, and when the child is tested with the challenges of life, he will remain within the way he has been trained, because of the reinforcement given in the home. The word "**train**" further means to create an environment that is conducive to life or one that will foster growth. The original meaning of the word "**parent**" means mother and father. The perfect will of God is that children be nurtured and instructed in righteousness by both the father and mother. Together, they are responsible for setting the tone and temperament of the home. Even if the child veers off for a season, the Godly training deposited within will draw him back. Parents must protect children from the seed of corruption.

At the writing of this book, I am the mother of two boys and one daughter. My daughter and I share many conversations. The peer pressure she undergoes, as well as all of our teenagers, is tremendous. She often tells me how her peers make mockery of her and tell her she is in prison, because she is not allowed to be a partaker of their worldly pleasures. However, she understands that her way is hedged up and governed by guidelines that will usher her into a life that is conducive to maximum fulfillment, free from the corruption that many young people are involved in, or exposed to.

When she is confronted with compromise, I am certain that the moral standards and Godly principles instilled within her will keep her and direct her, even though she is ridiculed by those she thought were her friends. The Godly wisdom we have invested in our children and the power of the Holy Ghost, is greater than every assault the devil launches against them.

Proverbs 22:15
*Foolishness is bound in the heart of a child; but
the rod of correction shall drive it far from him.*

Foolishness comes from a Hebrew word which means "perverseness". Because every child born has the nature of satan, perversion is bound up in them at birth. This is why our children must receive Jesus, live by divine order and be instructed in the ways of God. We must use the rod of correction to instruct them in the way of righteousness, until it becomes a way of life for them, a normal response.

Proverbs 23:13-14
Withhold not correction from the child: for if thou

beatest him with the rod, he shall not die. Thou shalt deliver his soul from hell.

Proverbs 13:24
He that spareth his rod hateth his son: but he that loveth him chasteneth him betimes.

If we love our children, we will not withhold chastening from them. If we refuse to chasten our children, God says we hate them and are doing them a great injustice. If we correct our children, we are preparing them to deal with life. They must adhere to authority and respect the laws of the land. Once learned at home, they will have no problems respecting authority away from home. If we refuse to discipline them or teach them how to respect authority domestically, the world is waiting for them, and without Godly training, our children will violate the laws of the land.

There is a difference in disciplining a child in love and abusing a child. Any parent who denies a child food, burns a child in hot water, or sticks a hot iron to a child's skin, is psychologically imbalanced and needs immediate help. It is because of this kind of abuse that the civil authorities question a parent's right to chastise children. If chastening is done in the proper manner and with love as the only motive, a spanking is not detrimental to the emotional well-being of a child, but is an extremely positive tool in rearing a child properly before God. This is an orderly arrangement, and it definitely proves advantageous when adhered to by God's standards.

God instructs the fathers to refrain from provoking their children or wounding their spirits. This is done by excessive abuse, verbally and physically. Parents must know that a spanking or punishment is not a remedy for all disobedience, and should create an environment for communication. Communication is effective when the parent not only talks, but can share in what the child is experiencing by listening and feeling as well. There must be understanding in the heart of what the child is experiencing and the child must know that the parent loves him or her with their best interest as a number one priority. Communication is not always verbal; it involves timing, tone, and touch. There must always be the proper time to talk, a soft tone and the ability to touch. Whenever we are too angry to touch, we are too angry to talk. Self-control and self-discipline are extremely important during these times.

the home. He never demands anything of his family. They freely give him the honor he deserves. This is God's divine order.

The wife has been given the position of authority in the realm of influence. There are instances in scripture when influence was more powerful than the position of authority. Influence is so powerful that it can persuade one in authority to make godly or ungodly decisions. This is why women must be filled with the Holy Ghost and submissive to the order of God. Women have influenced men for centuries and will continue to do so.

As mentioned earlier, the power of influence is clearly seen in the lives of Adam and Eve, Samson and Delilah, Ahab and Jezebel, Esther and many others.

If a woman is married to a man who is unsaved, she can still experience fulfillment in God. The Bible is not silent concerning unsaved authority.

I Corinthians 7:12-16

But to the rest speak I, not the Lord: if any brother hath a wife that believeth not, and she be pleased to dwell with him, let him not put her away. And the woman which hath a husband that believeth not, and if he be pleased to dwell with her, let her not leave him. For the unbelieving husband is sanctified by the wife, and the unbelieving wife is sanctified by the husband: else were your children unclean; but now are they holy. But if the unbelieving depart, let him depart. A brother or a sister is not under bondage in such cases: but God hath called us to peace. For what knowest thou, O wife, whether thou shall save thy husband? Or how knowest thou, O man, whether thou shall save thy wife?

I Peter 3:1-7

Likewise, ye wives, be in subjection to your own husbands; that, if any obey not the word, they also may without the word be won by the conversation of the wives; While they behold your chaste conversation coupled with fear. Whose adorning let it not be that outward adorning of plaiting the hair, and of wearing of gold, or of putting on of apparel; but let it be the hidden man of the heart, in that which is not corruptible, even the ornament of a meek and quiet spirit, which is in the sight of God of great price. For after this manner in the old time the holy women also, who trusted in God, adorned themselves, being in subjection unto their own husbands: Even as Sara obeyed Abraham, calling him lord: whose daughters ye are, as long as ye do well, and are not afraid with any amazement Likewise ye husbands, dwell with them according to knowledge, giving honour unto the wife, as unto the weaker vessel, and as being heirs together of the grace of life; that your prayers be not hindered.

The Bible says that the unsaved husband can be won, not by what his wife says, but how she lives before him. The wife must understand how to love her husband unconditionally, and remember that although her ultimate commitment and loyalty is to God, her ministry must be directed towards her husband, (ministry simply means to serve) because she is joined to the Lord, she is one spirit with Him, and **Jesus is her spiritual head**

I Corinthians 6:17
But he (inclusive of woman) that is joined unto the Lord is one spirit.

Proverbs 16:3
Commit thy works unto the Lord, and thy thoughts shall be established.

Proverbs 3:5-6
*Trust in the Lord with all thine heart; and lean
not unto thine own understanding. In all thy ways
acknowledge him, and he shall direct thy paths.*

As the wife submits to the Word of God, God will direct her
as to how to pray for her husband and make wise decisions in the
best interest of the relationship. Many marriages have ended in
divorce because women became too spiritual and self-absorbed
to realize that it is not a mandate from God to be in church every
time the doors are open, or to spend excessive time in prayer,
neglecting the basic needs of a marital relationship; such as
preparing dinner, cleaning the house, making love, etc. An
unsaved mate does not want his wife's pastor in bed with him or
always being the topic of discussion. Women must have balance
and wisdom in building their homes and relationships with their
husbands (and vice-versa). There are times when a wife should
just spend a quiet evening with her husband; not preaching to
him or attempting to pastor him, but love him, listen to him, and
encourage him.

God is more concerned about our loved ones being saved and
enjoying His plan for their lives than we are.

II Peter 3:9
*The Lord is not slack concerning his promise, as
some men count slackness; but is longsuffering
to usward, not willing that any should perish, but
that all should come to repentance.*

Acts 2:38-39
*Then Peter said unto them, repent, and be baptized
every one of you in the name of Jesus Christ for
the remission of sins, and ye shall receive the gift
of the Holy Ghost. For the promise is unto you,
and to your children, and to all that are afar off,
even as many as the Lord our God shall call.*

A woman can use the power of influence in a Godly manner to usher the plan of God into the life of her husband. She can be powerfully instrumental in the hands of God, if she will love her husband naturally, and pray for him spiritually, while living a morally excellent life before him. God majors in transforming what may appear to be a hopeless situation.

Romans 4:17-21

(As it is written, I have made thee a father of many nations,) before him whom he believed, even God, who quickeneth the dead, and calleth those things which be not as though they were. Who against hope believed in hope, that he might become the father of many nations, according to that which was spoken, so shall thy seed be. And being not weak in faith, he considered not his own body now dead, when he was about a hundred years old, neither yet the deadness of Sarah's womb: He staggered not at the promise of God through unbelief; but was strong in faith, giving glory to God; And being fully persuaded that, what he had promised, he was able also to perform.

James 4:7

Submit yourselves therefore to God. Resist the devil and he will flee from you.

The scripture above reveals the key to our continued success as the people of God. I want to show you how to avoid failure in every facet of your lives. I want to show you how you can win, win again, and keep on winning. Just in one word, today, I can show you how to always realize victory, no matter what the crisis; no matter what the challenge; no matter what the report. In one word today, I want to show you how, "it's not over, until you win."

Winning is God's idea; He is the ultimate winner and He only reproduces winners. He gives us the strategy by which to win all the time. Everybody wants to be on a winning team. If you have accepted Jesus Christ as Lord and Savior of your life, you made the decision to join a winning team. However, there are some steps we must take that are essential to a winner's success. Let's consider the steps by first looking at the key element. The key lies in the word **submit**.

Let's consider again what does submit mean. Submit comes from the Greek word, "hupeiko" and means to withdraw from and come under or yield (hupo means under-eiko means yield); to subject; the word subject comes from the Greek word "hupotasso;" To rank oneself under; to arrange under. Hupo means under, therefore the word "**submit**" simply means, to withdraw from disorder and position or arrange oneself under God. There is always order in God. God calls us out of disorder. When we submit to God we surrender totally to Him. We will never be able to overcome the forces of darkness, unless we totally surrender to God. We will never win unless we are properly aligned in God and with God. We must be in the place God ordained; He ranked us a little lower than Himself.

Psalm 8:4-8

What is man, that thou art mindful of him? And the son of man, that thou visitest him? For thou hast made him a little lower than the angels, and hast crowned him with glory and honor. Thou madest him to have dominion over the works of thy hands; thou hast put all thing under his feet:

God created man as the highest and most valuable in worth of all His creation. To say God is mindful of us means, He is "zakar," to mark or remember continually, to set the heart upon and be consumed with man's well-being. God is consumed with our success. He placed us in a winning position and deposited within us the capacity to win and keep on winning. His Son became a partaker of flesh and blood to ensure our success and seal the devil's defeat.

Colossians 1:12-13

Giving thanks unto the Father, which hath made us meet to be partakers of the inheritance of the saints in light: Who hath delivered us from the power of darkness, and hath translated us into the kingdom of his dear Son:

God has called us to submit to His order; a higher order; He called us out of darkness. Before a man or a woman can submit to one another, we must submit to God.

Ephesians 5:21

Submitting yourselves one to another in the fear of God.

Many times we are stubborn in our own opinions. This is only because we have not totally surrendered ourselves to God.

I Samuel 15:23 says, *stubbornness is as iniquity and idolatry.*

A stubborn person will always be an ignorant person. Why? Stubborn people are unteachable. They have a refusal to change.

Stubbornness means unpersuadable; obstinate rejection of the will of God; refusal to change; one who will not hear the voice of truth; one who becomes careless in attitude. Carelessness in attitude is the precursor of actual disobedience.

The devil will always seek to lure us into a place of disobedience; you and I will never know the joy of winning when we disobey God. God has called us away from iniquity and idolatry.

Iniquity is an offense against God and His holiness; lawlessness; unrighteousness; actions not in concert with or conformity to the Word of God; the opposite of righteousness.

Idolatry is sin of the mind against God; lack of the acknowledgment of God; absence of gratitude towards God; one who is a slave to the abased and the depraved lusts of the flesh.

Submission is a place of power in that one's life commands the respect of others. Why?

1. Because we know who we are. When we know who we are, we will not allow someone else's opinion of us to become our opinion of self. When we know who we are, we will take charge of our lives. When we know who we are, we will not allow anybody to define our:

   a. **worth** - our worth is defined by the God who made me. No man can put a price-tag on us. We don't sell cheap.

   b. **purpose** - our purpose is defined by the God who made me. No man can define purpose to us.

   c. **potential** - our potential is defined and designed by the God who made us; we will never be limited.

   d. **position** - our position is defined by the God who made me, I will not be a clone, or robot for anybody to mis-use, abuse, or defuse,

   e. **identity** - our identity is established by the God who made us, we will never accept a foreign identity.

When we know who we are, we will not ever conform to the norm. We will not conform to the world.

Romans 12:1-2

I beseech you therefore, brethren, by the mercies of God, that ye present your bodies a living sacrifice, holy, acceptable unto God, which is your reasonable service. And be not conformed to this world: but be ye transformed by the renewing of your mind, that ye may prove what is that good, and acceptable, and perfect, will of God.

When we know who we are, we maximize all the qualities God has given us.

God has placed woman in an awesome position in this earth. He has designed us to grace this earth with the emotions of God, the motherhood of God. He has given us the power of influence in this earth. Yes, man is the head of woman, he has been given the authority to oversee everything in this earth, and everything a woman does.

Genesis 2:18
And the Lord God said, it is not good that the man should be alone; I will make him an help meet for him.

Adam was not lonely. He was alone. There is a great difference between being alone and being lonely.

The state of singleness should be a goal for every individual. Singleness should be pursued, not avoided. The word **"single"** refers to wholeness, completion, and perfection, unique; having no equal; all of us married or unmarried should be single and enjoy singleness. We were born to win, but we can choose to lose. We can choose to walk through life thinking defeated, thinking like a loser, behaving like a loser, and feeling like a loser. When we feel like we need an individual, male or female, to make you complete, all of the forces of darkness will come to our aid. We are not submitted to God with this mindset. When we truly submit to God, we will understand the difference between **being alone** and **being lonely**:

Alone means without support or help; isolated.

Lonely means a strong feeling of being desolate; showing the effects of abandonment and neglect; dilapidated - partly ruined or decayed; lacking signs of life; lacking comfort or hope; gloomy; wasteful. ***Loneliness is a choice***.

God made all of us in His image and power packed us with the potential to achieve in a capacity that will boggle the minds of the people of this world. He has defined success as the God-given ability to accomplish pre-determined goals and dreams coupled with the capacity to experience fulfillment over the desired accomplishment. Wealth is who we are and our capacity to appreciate our value as we release the power God has placed within. We are unstoppable, unbeatable.

Success is never contingent upon the presence or absence of another individual. When we submit to God we will truly understand this.

When God saw Adam alone, He simply said there is no one to assist this man and help him become what he was formed to be, and only influence can help this man. I will put my influence in woman so he can succeed. A helpmeet is one who is suitable to man intellectually, spiritually, morally, and physically. One who is suitable and adaptable to the man. "Help" comes from the Hebrew word "azar," which means to assist, compliment; adapting to the designed purpose.

God knows men do not readily adapt to change. God made woman to readily adapt and change, to the purpose for which man was designed. The woman can change, so as to fit the need warranted by the situation. It doesn't matter who the man is, man cannot become successful in this earth without influence; without woman. Whether the influence comes from a wife, sister, aunt, grandmother, mother, or a professional, man need's female assistance. This is why it is vitally important that we all understood the power of submission.

The basic quality in womanhood is femininity. Femininity has as much strength as masculinity in its place. Femininity is that tender quality found in a woman's appearance, manner, and nature. A feminine woman gives the impression of softness and holiness. She has a spirit of sweet submission and a dependency upon the male for care and protection only within the confines of marriage. Women in ministry should never compete with men, or attempt to be masculine in their presentation of the Gospel. A woman is gentle, understanding, never loud and boisterous.

God created woman as the glory of man. We do not tear down and destroy our beauty with profanity, fowl movies, cigarettes, drugs, liquor, masturbation, lesbianism, and premarital sex. We represent womanhood and we need the strength of womanhood. Laying aside our femininity and taking on a masculine demeanor will weaken our ability and destroy the power of influence. There

is nothing masculine about the woman God created to represent
Him in the earth.

In order to truly understand the essence of womanhood and
celebrate the powerful position we hold in the eyes of God, we
consider God's divine intent as He fashioned us. He gave us
definition. Often we are looked upon as beings made to service
men, clean the house, take care of the clothes, prepare the meals,
take care of the children, and fulfill sexual fantasies.

On the contrary, God formed us for so much more. We are here
to ultimately give God glory as we bring our men to their highest
and best in the kingdom of God. We are here to fulfill God's will,
whether that be Pastor/Teacher, preacher, or housewife.

Womanhood is a daily process of developing all the feminine
qualities invested in us by an Almighty God so that, as His
influence in the earth, we are God ruled by our submission to
God. I love my husband and I am faithful to him, because of my
relationship with God. He is the benefactor of my relationship
with God. I believe I can achieve the impossible, because of my
relationship with God.

Chapter Four

Who Is the Spiritual Head of Woman?

The Apostle Paul wrote the epistles of first and second Corinthians primarily concerning Christian life and conduct. All the doctrinal sections of these epistles are built around this theme. The occasion for writing was due to a letter from the Corinthian church inquiring about challenges with regard to certain doctrines and customs.

I Corinthians 1:3
But I would have you know that the head of every man is Christ.

If a man is born into the family of God, he is under the authority of God. Headship refers to the immediate or principle influence of one over another, the one who sets the course, or direction of another by precept and example. God's Word is given to establish order in our lives. The husband, who is influenced by God, and yielded to God's Word, understands that he has relinquished his rights to guide his family by his own ingenuity. He must guide his family by living the Word before them, consistently and purposefully.

His submission to God and obedience to God initiates a positive response in the wife and children. He leads all members of the family, as he first walks in the ways of God before them. The husband is given to the wife to protect her from the forces of evil. He is there not to dominate and enslave her, but to bring her to a point of total fulfillment and spiritual development, as she walks with God and assists him in being all God has ordained him to be. The husband further protects the wife by leading her by influence. As he gets instruction from Christ, who is his head, he shares with his wife.

God influences Christ; Christ influences the man; the man influences the wife, and the husband and wife together influence the children into becoming all God has ordained them to be.

I Corinthians 3:4

Every man praying or prophesying having his head covered dishonored his head.

The Corinthian Church held to varied customs and traditions that had no spiritual significance whatsoever. They felt that if a man had a cap or any physical covering on his head while praying or prophesying, he disrespected Christ who is the Spiritual Head of the Church. Christ is not only the male-man's head, but Christ is the Head of every born again believer, the married and unmarried. If a woman is saved, in the family of God, single or married, Christ is her spiritual head. In the home, a married woman has her husband as the domestic or natural head. In the Body of Christ, Christ is the Head of the Church.

A born again wife of an unsaved man or an unmarried woman would have no spiritual head if man was the spiritual head of woman. Every man cannot stand in the same relationship to every woman as Christ does to every male-man and every female-man. Every man is not the head of every woman. A man may be the head of one woman—his wife, but he is not the head of every woman.

I Corinthians 6:17

But he (male and female) that is joined unto the Lord is one spirit.

Every woman can come to Christ directly without the consent or mediation of her husband. There are many women, unmarried and married, who are walking in closer fellowship with God then some men. Women do not have inferior roles in the Body of Christ, but in the home, the husband is the natural head. Yet, he and his wife are equal partners together in all that concerns the family unit. The husband was designed to shoulder the greater responsibility; therefore, he was placed in the position of authority. Christ, though eternally equal with God, took a subordinate position and was obedient to the will of God.

Philippians 2:5-8

Let this mind be in you, which was also in Christ Jesus: who, being in the form of God, thought it not robbery to be equal with God: but made himself of no reputation, and took upon him the form of a servant, and was made in the likeness of men: and being found in fashion as a man, he humbled himself, and became obedient unto death, even the death of the cross.

I Corinthians 3:5

But every woman that prayeth or prophesieth with her head uncovered dishoureth her head: for that is even all one as if she were shaven.

For years, the custom for women was that they be veiled. The clothing worn by the Hebrew people of Biblical times was graceful, modest, and extremely significant. Clothing told who they were and what they were. The woman's head-dress consisted of a cloth for covering the head. If a woman were married, elaborate ornaments and jewels were set within the veil to distinguish her marital position. Among the Greeks it was universal for women to appear in public with their heads covered. The veil was looked upon as the truest and most treasured emblem of a woman's position of subjection. Just as women today wear a wedding band, or wedding ring, showing that we are legally married, bonded to another.

Genesis 24:65

For she had said unto the servant, what man is this that walketh in the field to meet us? And the servant had said, it is my master: therefore she took a vail (veil), and covered herself.

Ruth 3:15

Also he said, bring the veil that thou hast upon thee, and hold it. And when she held it, he measured six measures of barley, and laid it on her: and she went into the city.

We can clearly see that the veil was a symbol of subjection to the husband. It distinguished a woman's position as being in covenant with her husband (in essence, it was a symbol of position).

The Rabbis and priests could not touch a woman in public nor instruct her in the scriptures in public. The wearing of veils was among other nations as a custom also. Only prostitutes or women of questionable character in the East went without veils. Therefore, for a woman to pray or prophesy without a veil would be identifying her with harlotry. Women who were harlots or who were caught in adultery were killed; this will be discussed further in another chapter. If a married woman appeared in public without a veil, she would disgrace her husband. It would be the same as women who had hair shaved off their head, which stated she was under-going punishment for whoredom, or caught in prostitution. Paul answers the questions of the Corinthian church in **I Corinthians 11:16**.

I Corinthians 11:7-16

For a man indeed ought not to cover his head, forasmuch as he is the image and glory of God: but the woman is the glory of the man. For the man is not of the woman; but the woman of the man. Neither was the man created for the woman; but the woman for the man. For this cause ought the woman to have power on her head because of the angels. Nevertheless neither is the man without the woman, neither the woman without the man, in the Lord. For as the woman is of the man, even so is the man also by the woman; but all things *of God. Judge in yourselves: is it comely that a woman pray unto God uncovered? Doth not even nature itself teach you, that, if a man have long hair, it is a shame unto him? But if a woman have long hair, it is a glory to her, for her hair is given her for a covering. But if any man seem to be contentious, <u>we have no such custom, neither the churches of God</u>.*

God put purpose in every woman; however, we have gleamed many erroneous beliefs from church, which have affected our thinking, attitude, and behavior concerning women in general. Many members in the family of God have been operating on false information. To say God does not use women in ministry is a lie. Perhaps the following information will assist us in understanding the position of man and woman in the Body of Christ. When God created mankind, both male and female, the plan for rulership and dominion was delegated to both male and female. However, in the Jewish culture, in both the Old and New Testament, woman is viewed as a second-rate citizen. For example, sons inherited land, but daughters received only maintenance. If a wife found anything, it belonged to her husband, as did the work of her hands. A woman's inheritance, should there be no male to receive it, could be used by her husband for his desires. A woman could not publicly learn in the synagogue. If she had a question, she would ask her husband when they got home. In Christ, the old forms of legalism and subjugation are done away with. Old inferiorities are eliminated.

Today, women recognize that we are established in righteousness even as the male through the blood of the Lord Jesus Christ. Today, male and female are subject to Christ once saved. Every woman, man and child has direct access to God, through Jesus Christ.

Chapter Five

Understanding the Protective Power of Authority

The Bible speaks of authority in three areas, the Church, Civil Government, and in the home. Jesus has all authority over mankind. His greatest joy is to use that authority to maximize the growth and development of those whom he had authority over. Every person on this earth must be subject to authority. The word "subject" means to yield to the rule of another or one who is brought under the control of another. One can be subject to authority willingly or by force. However, I will deal with the benefits of authority from God's perspective.

"Subjection" from God's perspective should be something we willingly do. Authority has been viewed as something that enslaves people and deprives them of true liberty. Nothing could be farther from the truth. There is protection in authority. The Greek word "EXOUSIA" has several meanings. It is used to illustrate "higher power," and is the right to influence or direct another. All authority comes from God and is ordained of God. Ordain means, "to place, to set, to appoint, to order, to set in order or in its proper arrangement or position."

Therefore, God sets the order for the authorities He has ordained and this will be proven by many of the scriptures used in this chapter.

We must all learn to respect authority and see it as the divine plan of God to protect our lives. Whenever you and I choose to resist authority, we become a hindrance to the order and plan of God Almighty.

Romans 13:2

Whosoever therefore resisteth the power, resisteth the ordinance of God: and they that resist shall receive to themselves damnation.

When we resist the authorities ordained of God, we are not resisting the authority, but we are resisting God. To resist God causes us to set in motion the consequences of our actions and forfeit the protective power of God. To resist authority is rebellion and God says rebellion is the sin of witchcraft. Rebellion stems from the conditions of a man's heart and mind. It is defiance against the order of God, or resistance to any form of authority.

A person can appear to be submissive outwardly, yet, have the root of rebellion within. God can only honor and reward us based upon what is within the heart.

Resistance to authority stems also from bitterness and pride. Knowing God, submitting to His Word, knowing who we are and respecting God's divine order are the keys to functioning successfully under authority. God gives us His Word to direct our lives. When we walk in the truth of God's Word, He gives illumination and revelation.

In order to stand in the position of authority, we must learn to operate within the framework of delegated authority. Authority employs the process of one winning devotion and allegiance from another, or the process of compelling the acceptance and trust of another. Many believers have a problem with submission, because of status and our own ambitions to achieve excellence or reputation for superiority. To put it simply, it is man's desire to rule, rather than be ruled. This mind-set is dangerous, because when our desires are not saturated with the Word of God, and balanced with yieldedness to the plan of God, we are open prey for the forces of darkness. If we cannot submit to authority, we cannot be trusted to rule over others.

Authority has been viewed with disdain in many arenas. Often, I believe we fail to consider what this world would be like without authority, what the home would be like, and what the church would be like. Every area of life will be strengthened and enhanced when the principles of authority are assimilated and respected.

As mentioned earlier, all authorities are ordained or appointed by God. It is God's plan that "Governments" exist to protect citizens and enforce civil laws. Have you ever wondered what life would be like without a president, the armed forces, police officers, mayors, congressmen, college professors and the like? These authorities and many others are ordained of God. However, God is not responsible for the corruption in people. He instituted the office for good. Men have perverted and corrupted the offices because of the evil within them as seen in greed, the thirst for power, position, fame and fortune.

All these exist when those in positions of authority have no relationship with God, or have a relationship, but are consumed with self, void of discipline in their lives and no genuine concept of mind and heart as to why God ordained the authority. Whenever the purpose of the office is not truly realized, the individual in the office will abuse the rights and privileges of the authority. God will judge all those who abuse the authority and the office that He has ordained for the good of men. Human government is instituted by God. The purpose is to enforce natural laws and natural order in this earth. As believers, we should have an automatic response of obedience as it pertains to respecting the laws of the land. We submit out of obedience to God and, therefore, enjoy the benefits of respecting authority.

God did not ordain authority, whether it is in government, in the home or in the church, to enslave His people or rob us of certain liberties, but to protect all men. Let's consider the following scripture:

I Peter 2:13-17

Submit yourselves to every ordinance of man for the Lord's sake: whether it be to king, as supreme; or unto governors, as unto them that are sent by him for the punishment of evildoers and for the

*praise of them that do well. For so is the will of
God, that with well doing ye may put to silence the
ignorance of foolish men: as free, and not using
your liberty for a cloke of maliciousness, but as
the servants of God. Honour all men. Love the
brotherhood. Fear God. Honour the king.*

Believers are encouraged in the above scripture to obey natural laws and civil rulers as long as they do not transgress the laws of God. We are admonished to subject ourselves to every human being who has any authority. We are to cooperate with them because they enforce the same mandates God has ordained every believer to live by. God has called the church to be the model for others in obeying the laws of the land, so that no unbeliever will be justified in bringing an accusation against the righteous.

In verse 15 above, God reveals that this is His will and that by the church's obedience; foolish men will be brought to shame and embarrassment. The scripture uses the word "ignorance" which comes from the Greek word "agnosia", which means the absence of true knowledge. True knowledge comes from God. Every believer has the responsibility to help establish and support human government for the preservation of society and promotion of the highest good of all men.

Romans 13:1-3

*Let every soul be subject unto the higher powers.
For there is no power but of God; the powers that
be are ordained of God. Whosoever therefore
resisteth the power, resisteth the ordinance of God:
and they that resist shall receive to themselves
damnation. For rulers are not a terror to good
works, but to the evil. Wilt thou then not be afraid
of the power? Do that which is good, and thou
shall have praise of the same:*

God plainly tells us that if we set ourselves against His plan in human government, we resist Him, not men. And if we resist

God, we will experience consequences. Civil rulers are not in positions of authority to terrorize men of character and integrity, but to punish evil men for sins against society. God has delegated governmental authority to defend the righteous and God-fearing, and also to punish the evil.

During the Old Testament, people who violated God's order in government, the home or the church were killed. If a man raped a woman or if a man and woman were caught in adultery, they were stoned. If a person was kidnapped, the person doing the kidnapping was killed. If a virgin committed fornication, she was killed. Rebellious children were killed. For those who doubt these statements, consider the following:

Deuteronomy 22:20-27

But if this thing be true, and the tokens of virginity be not found for the damsel: then they shall bring out the damsel to the door of her father's house, and the men of her city shall stone her with stones that she die: because she hath wrought folly in Israel, to play the whore in her father's house: so shall thou put evil away from among you. If a man be found lying with a woman married to an husband, then they shall both of them die, both the man that lay with the woman, and the woman: so shall thou put away evil from Israel. If a damsel that is a virgin be betrothed unto an husband, and a man find her in the city, and lie with her; then ye shall bring them both out unto the gate of that city, and ye shall stone them with stones that they die; the damsel, because she cried not, being in the city; and the man, because he hath humbled his neighbor's wife: so thou shall put away evil from among you. But if a man find a betrothed damsel in the field, and the man force her, and lie with her: then the man only that lay with her shall die: But unto the damsel thou shall do nothing;

there is in the damsel no sin worthy of death: for as when a man riseth against his neighbor, and slayeth him, even so is this matter: for he found her in the field, and the betrothed damsel cried, and there was none to save her.

Deuteronomy 21:18-23

If a man have a stubborn and rebellious son, which will not obey the voice of his father, or the voice of his mother, and that, when they have chastened him, will not hearken unto them: then shall his father and his mother lay hold on him, and bring him out unto the elders of his city, and unto the gate of his place; and they shall say unto the elders of his city, this our son is stub-born and rebellious, he will not obey our voice; he is a glutton, and a drunkard. And all the men of his city shall stone him with stones, that he die: so shall thou put evil away from among you; and all Israel shall hear, and fear. And if a man have committed a sin worthy of death, and he be put to death, and thou hang him on a tree: His body shall not remain all night upon the tree, but thou shall in any wise bury him that day; (for he that is hanged is accursed of God;) that thy land be not defiled, which the Lord thy God giveth thee for an inheritance.

I Timothy 1:8-10

But we know that the law is good, if a man use it lawfully; knowing this, that the law is not made for a righteous man, but for the lawless and disobedient, for the ungodly and for sinners, for unholy and profane, for murderers of fathers and murderers of mothers, for manslayers, whoremongers, for them that defile them-selves with mankind, for menstealers, for liars, for

perjured persons, and if there be any other thing
that is contrary to sound doctrine;

I must reiterate that every believer has a responsibility to help bring about the best government to secure the highest good of all. Human governments are established by divine order to insure the needs of humanity in securing our highest good. If in a small family law and penalties are needed how much more are they needed in communities, states, and nations? When government is corrupt, believers must pray for reform.

It is the responsibility of every believer to pursue moral excellence and teach their children to demand the same of themselves. Righteousness is perpetuated in the family of God, when believers are morally excellent and pass this same conviction and responsibility on to future generations. Government can enforce natural obedience, but not spiritual obedience. The highest order of obedience is that which is spiritual. Obedience to God should be paramount in our lives.

Upon the grounds of the best public interests, it becomes the duty of human governments to use all necessary means to attain this end. It is absurd to believe that rulers have the right to use the necessary means to carry on good government. Such error or belief causes many believers to object to the right to capital punishment, the right to deal with gangs, to suppress rebellions, and to make wars on criminal nations. Authorities are ordained to suppress rebellion and enforce respect for law and order. God has established divine order in civil matters.

Rulers are God's servants to execute proper judgment upon the ungodly, and preserve moral excellence for the good of all. Since we have clearly examined the authority ordained of God as it pertains to civil government, let's now examine the order of government God has instituted for the family. *"**Exousia**"* we stated, means the power of influence or command freedom granted by one who is in authority in behavior. God has given us authority and this authority has as its chief end protection for all who seek to understand and submit.

Children need authorities to guide, develop, and strengthen them. Adults fulfill their prospective roles when they function fully within family government. We have come to fear the influence of authority as a threat to our liberties in the family; however, God granted man the power of authority and woman has the power of influence. Each compliments the other. There is a crucial need for authority in family government. Many of our children have veered off because of improper authority in the home, or the lack of authority. Before they could ever respect or adhere to civil authority, they must have learned respect and adherence to authority in the home.

God has called us to be subject to one another in love. Authority is not to be perceived as a threat to our freedom, but as the protective umbrella of covering that defines our borders and keeps us from straying into a place of grave danger. Submission to authority, when it is understood, becomes an attitude of the heart. As I stated earlier, outward acts of submission do not constitute true submission. If a child performs everything that is expected of him, but if his heart is rebellious and he is thinking bitter thoughts towards the parent, he is not truly submitted and does not understand submission or authority. Remember, God considers the condition of the heart over outward acts or appearance.

A child who disobeys parental authority is really disobeying God. All authority that exists has been ordained by God. When we resist authority, we are, in essence, resisting God. The only exception is when an earthly authority is opposing God. Then we are to submit to God as the **"ULTIMATE AUTHORITY."** This is why a woman is under no obligation to stay with a husband who beats her physically or verbally. She is not required to yield to abuse or perverted requests. Neither are children required to be subject to a parent who resorts to pouring boiling water on them or cutting them with knives. These things are happening and are an abomination before Almighty God.

I fully realize that many people have abused the authority delegated them, but we cannot judge every person or office by the abuse of others. Many of us fail to understand that proper use of authority is best defined in the role of servitude. The person in authority actually becomes a servant to those entrusted into his or her care. God ordained authority not for the purpose of men ruling men but to establish order in our lives and protection.

Every entity is strengthened, organized and protected when the principles of authority have been assimilated. Success, fulfillment, and development are benefits enjoyed when authority is properly implemented, received, and respected. Whenever authority does not exist, anarchy reigns. Anarchy is defined as "the absence of law and order, a general state of disorder and confusion." If a father does not exercise dominion in his home, the wife may assume the leadership, taking the matriarchal role. Matriarchy is a design in the family, tribe, or other form of society in which the mother is ruler, with descent and succession being traced through her rather than the father. If the mother does not assume authority, the child will. Neither the child, nor the wife was ever designed to assume the authority in the home. They become the illegitimate heirs to the throne.

A legitimate personal authority is able to oversee because of experience, knowledge, and the ability to decide on the quality, value, or extent of a prized family relationship. The parent must give new confidence or courage to comfort the child or children. God can and does bless women who are parenting children without a husband (father) but this is not God's perfect will. Authority in the family government provides security and protection. This connotes the establishment of divine rank and order in every sphere. Those who embrace anarchy, rejecting the umbrella of authority, become lawless, seeking to make themselves as God.

Authority brings protection. Every person on this planet must be subject to someone, either by choice or by force. Those who refuse to acknowledge the protocol of authority always experience devastating consequences. God has given us His Word in order that we may understand authority as He has designed. The parameter of authority by which God has ordained us to function in and by brings lasting peace and rewards. To be under authority is a honor and requires that one have allegiance to another. God has established the government by which every man should adhere. We have examined the political government. Let's now examine the proper order for the family.

Authority inspires, by its behavior, others to follow. In the family, God has placed the husband as the responsible authority, domestically. The wife submits to the husband as unto the Lord and the husband submits to Christ as both submit to one another. The children submit to the parents. Children need authorities to guide, discipline, develop, protect, train, and reassure them. Many fear the influence of authority because of the abuse or negligence enforced by some. Authority should extend liberty and never enslave or hold captive. Authority is necessary and if we are to reap its benefits, we must understand how it is to operate.

As we have seen in the political offices and in many police officers, whenever there is improper use of authority, brutality, injustice and so much more will run rampant. Authority is not to be viewed as a threat to freedom, but as the protective umbrella of covering that defines life's boundaries and keeps us from the devastating consequences of lack of proper covering or protection. All authority that exists has been ordained by God; therefore, when we resist Authority, we are, in essence, resisting God. The only exception is when an earthly people opposes God. Then we are to submit to God as the highest power.

Wherever authority does not exist, then there is the absence of law and order. If there is no order, we can safely conclude that chaos is evident and when there is disorder or chaos, we will always find confusion and frustration. In the home the wife nor the child was designed to assume the authority in the home. For order's sake, God ordained the man to operate as the authority to protect his wife and children. The wife is given the power of influence to assist the husband, but she subjects herself to him fully assured that he is there to protect her spiritually, physically and emotionally.

The husband also assumes the role of providing and caring for his family. The children are instructed to subject themselves to the parents. What a lawless and chaotic situation if the child told the parents what to do. God established the positions in the home; anything otherwise becomes a disaster.

Chapter Six

God's Order for the Body of Christ

The church is identified as female in gender. We are the Bride of Christ; the "Ecclesia," the called out ones, and because we belong to God, He has established the order by which we are to operate as His Body in the earth. Man is not the head of God's church. ***Jesus is the head of the church.***

Ephesians 1:22-23
And hath put all things under his feet, and gave Him to be the Head over all things to the church, which is his body, the fulness of him that filleth all in all.

Ephesians 4:15
But speaking the truth in love, may grow up into him in all things, which is the head, even Christ:...

Ephesians 5:23
For the husband is the head of the wife, even as <u>*Christ is the head of the church*</u>*: and he is the savior of the body.*

Colossians 1:18
And he is the head of the body, the church: who is the beginning, the firstborn from the dead; that in all things he might have the pre-eminence.

The above scriptures clearly depict the position of Christ over the church. In **Ephesians 5:23**, the Bible draws a parallel by stating even as the husband is the natural authority over his wife in a domestic setting, so is Christ the authority over the church, which includes male and female.

Since Christ is the authority over the Church, then it should be clear that He can use whomever He chooses to proclaim the truth of the gospel in this earth whether male or female. He is no respecter of persons as it relates to His promises, provisions, plans, and purposes for every member of the Body. He reserves the right to select certain people to fulfill specific assignments in this earth.

When we consider God's order for the Body, we must examine and interpret scripture in light of what other scriptures on the same topic say. All scripture must harmonize with all scripture on the subject matter. As stated earlier in this book, much error has been perpetuated in the Body of Christ because many have ignored the law of proper scripture interpretation. Some misinterpretation of scripture has come about because many fail to realize there are historical, cultural and language differences separating Bible times from our times. There are certain principles or rules that must be adhered to in order to properly interpret the Bible. The Holy Spirit is the agent who gives us illumination (understanding). A misinterpretation of scripture can pass from one generation to another if we are not careful and serious students of the God's Word. We cannot depend on others alone, to give us a correct interpretation of scripture. We must stay in God's Word for ourselves.

We can have confidence in God to guide us if we are willing to always interpret scripture in its literal sense unless the context clearly indicates otherwise. We should never attempt to interpret scripture out of the carnality of our own minds. Neither should we attempt to arrive at some deep revelation based upon our own inflated ego. God has made His Word plain and simple. His Word must be spiritually discerned, yet it provides practical principles for practical living.

I Corinthians 2:14-15
But the natural man receiveth not the things of the Spirit of God: for they are foolishness unto him: neither can he know them, because they

are spiritually discerned. But he that is spiritual judgeth all things, yet he himself is judged of no man.

In order to properly interpret scripture, we must understand that the Bible is truth without error and there are no contradictions in the Bible. Contradiction is the end result when we fail to interpret scripture within its context; when we refuse to consider the historical and cultural setting, when we refuse to allow the Holy Spirit to illuminate truth to us and when we choose to hold on to religious beliefs imbedded in us by those we respect, even though what we were taught may have been incorrect.

We can make scriptures serve our own private agendas when we extract them from their context and refuse to seriously study Biblical history for ourselves.

A clear and concise understanding of correct word usage and meaning is also essential to correct scripture interpretation. Words are powerful carriers and are the essential elements by which we communicate. In order to understand what others are saying, we must have a basic knowledge of word usage. Bible scholars estimate that about 400 words have changed meaning from the way they were used in the King James Bible. Some words change meaning in a short period of time. A good example of understanding correct word usage is when we use the word "conversation" to refer to someone's speech, or a discussion between two or more people. However, in several passages of scripture, the word "conversation" refers to manner of living or lifestyle, behavior or conduct.

Psalm 50:23

Whoso offereth praise glorifieth me: and to him that ordereth his <u>conversation</u> aright will I shew the salvation of God.

Philippians 1:27

Only let your <u>conversation</u> be as it becometh the gospel of Christ: that whether I come and see you,

or else be absent, I may hear of your affairs, that
ye stand fast in one spirit, with one mind striving
together for the faith of the gospel;...

Conversation in the above verses refers to lifestyle; manner of living, conduct.

We can also consider the following:

Psalm 68:11 (KJV)

The Lord gave the word: great was the company
of those that published it.

Psalm 68:11 (Isaac Leeser Translation)

The Lord gave happy tidings, they are published
by the female messengers a numerous host.

Psalm 68:11 is a prophetic Psalm. Many Biblical scholars who oppose women in ministry will not expound on the fact that the Hebrew word translated "company" is feminine. It is not just a word referencing feminine gender, but it actually means women. This should not alarm anyone especially as we note the following scriptures:

John 20:1

The first day of the week cometh Mary Magdalene early, when it was yet dark, unto the sepulchre, and seeth the stone taken away from the sepulchre.

John 20:17

Jesus saith unto her, touch me not; for I am not yet ascended to my Father: but go to my brethren, and say unto them, I ascend unto my Father, and your Father; and to my God, and your God.

The first to go tell the men of the resurrection of Jesus was a woman. Jesus will use whatever vessel yields to Him whether male or female to spread the good news. The gospel is good news and preaching is simply telling or proclaiming the good news of the Gospel.

I Corinthians 1:26-29

For ye see your calling, brethren, how that not many wise men after the flesh, not many mighty, not many noble, are called: But God hath chosen the foolish things of the world to confound the wise; and God hath chosen the weak things of the world to confound the things which are mighty; And base things of the world, and things which are despised, hath God chosen, yea, and things which are not, to bring to nought things that are: that no flesh should glory in His presence.

Acts 10:34

Then Peter opened his mouth, and said, of a truth I perceive that <u>God is no respecter of persons</u>.

In first century Palestine, the way Jesus treated women was considered revolutionary. Jesus' honor and respect for women is portrayed throughout scripture. His attitude toward women was unexpected and unheard of in his culture and historical setting. Jesus, unlike the men of His generation and culture, taught that women were equal to me in the sight of God. Women received God's forgiveness, grace, and power. They could be personal followers of Christ and could be full participants in the Kingdom of God being established in this earth. Often we highlight the men who followed Jesus, but many women followed Jesus as well.

Mary of Magdala, known as Mary Magdalene **(Luke 8:2)** followed Jesus along with the male disciples.

Women were not allowed to be legal witnesses in court cases, but Jesus chose a woman to birth him in this earth, and he chose women as the first witnesses of His resurrection. They were the first to tell the good news. Women were called to be disciples of Jesus, just as men were and are expected to fulfill their spiritual responsibility just as men.

Jesus' ministry to Mary and Martha reveals that women were just as responsible for growing in grace and knowledge as men when it comes to being His followers. Martha invited Jesus to their home for a meal. But while she was busy preparing to serve Jesus, Mary was listening to Jesus expound on the Word. Jesus expected women as we as men to learn from Him. In view of the customs of the day what do you think would have happened if Jesus started calling the women instead of twelve men? In view of how the husbands looked upon their wives, imagine the chaos if He had said, "Women, leave your husbands, children, businesses and follow me." Can you imagine what the men would have done? Jesus came to establish order, not destroy relationships. Old biases must be put aside; the feelings of superiority over others must end. What God desires to do in and through all men (male and female) must be of paramount importance. Jesus frees all of us from satan's debilitating spiritual, physical, and emotional afflictions.

Women traveled with Jesus and **Luke 8:1-3**, says they ministered to Jesus out of their substance. A fascinating scripture which reveals Jesus' compassion for women is found in **Luke 13:10-13** where Jesus heals a woman on the Sabbath in the synagogue in front of the religious rulers. The healing not only shows Christ personally contrasting his new life with the old legalistic, pharisaic restrictions, but it also reveals his deep regard for women. The ruler of the synagogue protested and Jesus calls him a hypocrite. Jesus masters in elevating women to a new status in life.

Although Christ worked within the cultural traditions of the first century, he ignored the limitations that had been placed on women by the culture. Women were free to follow him and to take part in His ministry to the world.

Women cannot be excluded from ministry today, because Jesus made sure reference to their importance in ministry was documented:

Genesis 15:20

And Miriam the prophetess, the sister of Aaron, took a timbrel in her hand; and all the women went out after her with timbrels and with dances.

Judges 4:4

And Deborah, a prophetess, the wife of Lapidoth, she judged Israel at that time.

II Kings 22:14-15

So Hilkiah the priest, and Ahikam, and Achbor, and Shaphan, and Asahiah, went unto Huldah the prophetess, the wife of Sail urn the son of Tikvah, the son of Harhas, keeper of the wardrobe; (now she dwelt in Jerusalem in the college;) and they communed with her. And she said unto them, thus saith the Lord God of Israel, tell the man that sent you to me....

Nehemiah 6:14

My God, think thou upon Tobiah and Sanballat according to these their works, and on the prophetess Noadiah, and the rest of the prophets, that would have put me in fear.

Isaiah 8:3

And I went unto the prophetess; and she conceived, and bare a son...

Luke 2:36

And there was one Anna, a prophetess, the daughter of Phanuel, of the tribe of Aser: she was of a great age, and had lived with an husband seven years from her virginity; and she was a widow of about four-score and four years (84), which departed not from the temple, but served God with fastings and prayers night and day. And she coming in that instant gave thanks likewise unto the Lord, and spake of him to all them that looked for redemption in Jerusalem.

Acts 21:8-9

And the next day we that were of Paul's company departed, and came unto Caesarea: and we entered into the house of Philip the evangelist, which was one of the seven; and abode with him. And the same man had <u>four daughters, virgins, which did prophesy</u>.

Luke 24:10-11

It was Mary Magdalene, and Joanna, and Mary the mother of James, and other women that were with them, <u>which told these things unto the apostles. And their words seemed to them as idle tales, and they believed them not</u>.

Joel 2:28

And it shall come to pass afterward, that I will pour out my spirit upon all flesh; and your sons and your daughters shall prophesy, your old men shall dream dreams, your young men shall see visions.

Acts 2:17

And it shall come to pass in the last days, saith God, I will pour out of my Spirit upon all flesh: and your sons and your daughters shall prophesy, and your young men shall see visions, and your old men shall dream dreams:

In all of the passages above God used women to instruct others in spiritual things. In **Luke 24:10-11** we see that the apostles did not have confidence in what the women told them. However, the women spoke the truth. In **Joel 2:28 and Acts 2:17** God promises that He would pour out His Spirit upon women and they would prophesy. To prophesy means to speak to mankind to edification, exhortation, and comfort. Prophesying is ordained by God for the church, and in order for a woman to prophesy, she must open her mouth and speak. Surely Paul would not contradict God. Therefore, we must conclude that Paul was addressing another issue in **I Corinthians 14:34-35**. He was not referring to the preaching of the gospel or prophesying, but he was referring to the isolated disturbance in church services in the church of Corinth. He was referring to loud outbursts and questions that had nothing to do with the gospel message.

Many have asked, "Should women pastor?" Let's examine the question in light of God's Word.

I Timothy 3:1-7

This is a true saying, If a man desire the office of a bishop, he desireth a good work. A bishop then must be blameless, the husband of one wife, vigilant, sober, of good behaviour, given to hospitality, apt to teach; not given to wine, no striker, not greedy of filthy lucre; but patient, not a brawler, not covetous; one that ruleth well his own house, having his children in subjection with all gravity; (tor if a man know not how to rule his own house, how shall the take care of the church of God?) Not a novice, lest being lifted up with pride he fall into the condemnation of the devil. Moreover he must have a good report of them, which are without; lest he fall into reproach and the snare of the devil.

As we have learned from other passages of scripture, many verses in the Bible speak generically. Such as, "If any man be in Christ", or "If any man would come after me;" so it is with the above scripture. Even though the word "man" is used, it can refer to male or female. The word bishop comes from the Greek word "**episkope**" which means overseer, a preaching elder or one who proclaims truth.

Personally, I have been licensed and ordained. I am a married woman. I am a wife of one husband and our home life is in order. Our children are in subjection to us.

I have a husband who has done more to encourage me in ministry than any other person. He respects the call of God on my life and has never tried to interfere with God's purpose for my life. He makes every attempt to be present when I have to teach or preach. He encourages me to study and pray and creates an environment by which this is possible. While I am preaching, he receives God's Word just as eagerly as many others without reservation. Everywhere I go, I have peace within and peace with God because he freely supports me. I believe one of the most powerful reasons I am free to be all God called me to be as a wife, mother, a woman in ministry, and in particular, a pastor of growing church, is because of who he is, and how he motivates me to excel in ministry. Both Jerry and I understand what God is doing. The wisdom is that I am not so spiritual that I refuse to clean our home, wash our clothes, prepare our meals, nurture and invest time in my children, and be a wife to him as my husband.

I've had to go over homework assignments, prepare lunches, work as a full-time pastor, exercise, and do all the things that most women do. I respect my husband and submit to him as the natural authority in our home. I respect the call of God upon my family.

There are certain practices that Jerry and I are guarded against. One practice in particular, will be highly disputed by some, but we have clear and concise direction from the Spirit of God as to how our lives must be governed. The much disputed practice is the widely accepted co-pastorship. We have no scriptural base to accept this practice and strongly advise against such. In the Body of Christ, God gives Pastors to feed members of the local church with knowledge and understanding.

Jeremiah 3:15

And I will give you pastors according to mine heart, which shall feed you with knowledge and understanding.

A pastor has the responsibility of feeding God's people with the Word of God in full measure. Pastors are ordained of

God to nurture the flock to full development free of deception and manipulation. The Pastor may have an assistant or several assistants but he or she is the "ULTIMATE AUTHORITY", under God, over the flock.

I Peter 5:1-3

The elders (whether male or female) which are among you I exhort, who am also an elder, and a witness of the sufferings of Christ, and also a partaker of the glory that shall be revealed: feed the flock of God which is among you, taking the oversight thereof, not by constraint, but willingly; not for filthy lucre, but of a ready mind; neither as being lords over God's heritage, but being examples to the flock

God never ordained co-pastorship. Just because a man or woman is called and anointed to pastor, does not automatically mean the spouse is co-pastor. Many husbands and many wives have been forced into positions they are not called of God to fulfill. This title of co-pastor, has been acclaimed by many as the pattern by which the church is to operate. As a result, many relationships have been destroyed and many ministries have become ineffective, because the membership is not sure who is the "authority." Yes, husbands and wives should work together as partners and team players in ministry; however, my being married to a Pastor does not automatically make me a pastor. My being married to a Pastor simply means I am to do all I can to assist as my spouse maximizes all God has deposited in him for the full development of every member of the local church. I assume the responsibility of doing all I can to build the work of God and thereby, maximize the gift and deposit of God in my own life.

I not only represent Christ. I represent the Pastor by virtue of the fact that I am in a marital covenant. Submission to authority is not a struggle; it is an honor. The church is then perfectly aligned with God and all members submit to the visible authority.

Before one ever holds a position of authority, he or she must first learn submission. The degree by which we are willing to submit will always determine the degree of authority with which we will be entrusted. When authority is visible, concise, and the purpose defined, I believe people willingly align themselves to the order of God. The awesome insight into this truth is that a person, who cannot submit to authority, will never rise to authority. In Christ, we are all children of God, and we are all under authority when we submit to the Lordship of Jesus Christ.

Matthew 20:25-28

... Ye know that the princes of the Gentiles exercise dominion over them, and they that are great exercise authority upon them. But it shall not be so among you: but whosoever will be great among you, let him be your minister; and whomever will be chief among you, let him be your servant: even as the Son of man came not to be ministered unto, but to minister, and to give his life a ransom for many.

Chapter Seven

Qualification for Ministry

This book has nothing to do with Women's Liberation or Feminist Movements. This book has everything to do with the power of God being channeled through whomever He chooses. It is written to exhort women who are not trying to be men, but women who appreciate and value their femininity and are proud of their gender. It is written to inspire those who long to be all God ordained them to be. I believe the women God is raising up are chaste, discreet, wise, and humble. I believe they love and honor their husbands if they are married, and if unmarried I believe they are morally excellent.

Women truly called by God, are respecters of authority, because we are obedient to God. The truth that cannot be denied is that men have not been placed on planet earth to handle kingdom business alone. Men cannot successfully handle the affairs of God without women. This is not because women are more anointed or extremely gifted, but because God has orchestrated His own design by which His kingdom is established in this earth. He included women in His plan to reach the lost. Yes, there are many questions surrounding female leadership in the local church and the answers lie with an omniscient God who knows exactly what He is doing and cannot make a mistake.

God's plan to reach mankind must be influenced by a woman, even as His plan to redeem mankind was channeled through a woman. I am persuaded that if He sent His son to die for man, there are no limits to what He will do to extend man or a male-man is His business, and His alone. I charge the critics to consider the results and refrain from speaking evil against women in ministry lest they find themselves fighting against God.

Acts 5:35-39

And said unto them, ye men of Israel, take heed to yourselves what ye intend to do as touching these men. For before these days rose up Theudas, boasting himself to be somebody; to whom a number of men, about tour hundred, joined themselves: who was slain; and all, as many as obeyed him, were scattered, and brought to naught. After this man rose up Judas of Galileo in the days of the taxing, and drew away much people after him: he also perished; and all, even as many as obeyed him, were dispersed. And now I say unto you, refrain from these men, and let them alone; for if this counsel or this work be of men, it will come to naught: But if it be of God, ye cannot overthrow it; lest haply ye be found even to fight against God.

I Samuel 26:9

And David said to Abishai, destroy him not: for who can stretch forth his hand against the Lord's anointed, and be guiltless

Paul wrote the following Galatian Epistle from Rome. Galatia was not a city, but a providence, comprised of the churches at Antioch, Lystra, Iconium, and Derbe. He wrote this epistle to correct the thinking of new believers who were backsliding and following the teachings of false teachers. He wanted to set them straight regarding the relationship of Christians of the New Covenant with the Jesus of the Old Covenant. As it pertains to the church Paul says,

Galatians 3:26-28

For ye are all the children of God by faith in Christ Jesus. For as many of you as have been baptized into Christ have put on Christ. There is neither Jew nor Greek, there is neither bond nor

free, there is neither male nor female; for ye are
all one in Christ Jesus.

It is God who initiates the call and equips us for ministry. We must be sure our lives reflect the standard of righteousness established for us by the Word of God **(I Corinthians 1: 9-11).**

Romans 11:29
For the gifts and calling of God are without
repentance

There are certain qualifications that must be evident in every believer's life, whether the believer is in ministry or not. Our lives are held out for others to read, see, and know the power of God in visible demonstration **(Titus 1:5-10).** Every believer is called to ministry. Ministry is servitude and the best interest of God's people must take priority over everything else.

II Corinthians 3:6
Who also hath made us able ministers of the new
testament; not of the letter, but of the spirit: for
the letter killeth, but the spirit giveth life.

I Timothy 1:11-12
According to the glorious gospel of the blessed
God, which was committed to my trust. And I
thank Christ Jesus our Lord, who hath enabled
me, for that He counted me faithful, putting me
into the ministry (service to mankind.)

The standard by which we examine ourselves, our decisions, our relationships, and everything that we do, is God's Word.

Ephesians 5:1-2
Be ye therefore followers (mimetes—mimic in
all ways) of God, as dear children; and walk in
love, as Christ also hath loved us, and hath given
himself for us, and hath given himself for us an

offering and a sacrifice to God for a sweetsmelling savour.

I Thessalonians 4:1-7

Furthermore then we beseech you, brethren, and exhort you by the Lord Jesus, that as ye have received of us how ye ought to walk and to please God, so ye would abound more and more. For ye know what commandments we gave you by the Lord Jesus. For this is the will of God, even your sanctification, that ye should abstain from fornication; that every one of you should know how to possess his vessel in sanctification and honour; Not in the lust of concupiscence, (strong desire, not just for sex) even as the Gentiles which know not God: That no man go beyond and defraud his brother in any matter because that the Lord is the avenger of all such, as we also have forewarned you and testified. For God hath not called us unto uncleanness, but unto holiness.

I Timothy 3:1-7

This is a true saying, If a man desire the office of a bishop (episkopos, overseer) he desireth a good work. A bishop then must be blameless, the husband of one wife, vigilant, sober, of good behavior, given to hospitality, apt to teach (keenly intelligent) not given to wine, no striker, not greedy of filthy lucre (monetary gain); but patient, not a brawler (loud, quarrelsome) not covetous; one that ruleth well his own house, having his children in subjection with all gravity (semnotes=dignity); for if a man know not how to rule his own house, how shall he take care of the church of God. Not a novice, lest being lifted up with pride he fall into the condemnation of the devil. Moreover he must

have a good report of them, which are without;
lest he fall into reproach and the snare of the devil.

As ministers of the gospel, we must always control the flesh. Why? We must be willing to protect the anointing on our lives. We must never expose ourselves to anything that would contaminate our witness, and we must keep our fellowship with our Father intact, as we resist allowing any sin to enter our lives.

II Corinthians 4:7
But we have this treasure in earthen vessels, that the excellency of the power may be of God, and not of us.

We are living epistles. The most powerfully effective sermon is not the one we preach, but the one we live daily.

I Thessalonians 5:22
Abstain from all appearance of evil.

I Corinthians 9:27
But I keep under my body, and bring it into subjection: lest that by any means, when I have preached to others, I myself should be a castaway.

II Corinthians 3:3
Forasmuch as ye are manifestly declared to be the epistle of Christ ministered by us, written not with ink, but with the Spirit of the living God; not in table of stone, but in fleshy tables of the heart.

Acts 24:16
And herein do I exercise (Greek word is "askeo", to practice as an art) myself, to have always a conscience void of offense towards God and man.

Act 24:16 (Amplified)
I always exercise and discipline myself, mortifying the deeds of my body, deadening my carnal

appetites, bodily appetites and worldly desires, endeavoring in all respects to have a clear, unshaken, blameless conscience void of offense towards God or man.

As instruments in the hands of God, to affect the lives of others eternally, God requires that we have pure hearts, a good conscious, and sincere faith. He further requires that we be doctrinally sound **(II Timothy 2:15).** As we study, God will reveal His heart to us.

Amos 3:7
Surely the Lord God will do nothing but he revealeth his secret unto his servants the prophets.

What God has called us to do is greater than we are. Our dependence must be on Him. Many have a passion for titles and offices**, _but not_** a sincere desire to fulfill what is in the heart of God. We must love people, and we must know we are called to serve, not to be served.

I Timothy 1:15-16
This is a faithful saying, and worthy of all acceptation, that Christ Jesus came into the world to save sinners; of whom I am chief. Howbeit for this cause I obtained mercy, that in me first, Jesus Christ might shew forth all long-suffering, for a <u>pattern to them which should hereafter believe on him to life everlasting</u>.

We will never enjoy the fullness of God's anointing in our lives if we attempt to preach and teach lessons for which we have not first allowed God to perfect in us. As God perfects us and prepares us for ministry, we must respect His timing. Many ministries and ministers have died prematurely all because they dared to rush into ministry, without allowing God to perfect some things within them first. With what God has called us to do there is an appointed time. Grace is measured out for the gift; however, the grace to carry out the call is not activated until the season God has ordained for us to go forth.

Galatians 4:4

But when the fullness (pleroo in the Greek means to fill, satisfy, complete) of the time was come, God set forth his Son, made of a woman, made under the law...

Ecclesiastics 3:1

To every thing there is a season, and a time to every purpose under the heaven.

We must have clear insight into what God is calling us to do in ministry. He alone is obligated to ensure that His purpose for our lives is expressly clear and only He knows the season by which we are prepared to begin. Premature entry can prove devastating. It's okay to allow patience to be perfected within us. God will use the local authority set over us (our pastor) to release us at the appointed time.

Acts 13:1-3

Now there were in the church that was at Antioch certain prophets and teachers; as Barnabas, and Simeon that was called Niger, and Luc'ius of Cyrene, and Manaen which had been brought up with Herod the tetrarch, and Saul. As they ministered to the Lord, and fasted, the Holy Ghost said, separate me Barnabas and Saul for the work whereunto I have called them. And when they had fasted and prayed, and laid their hands on them, they sent them away.

John 1:16

And of his fullness have all we received, and grace for grace. For the law was given by Moses, but grace and truth came by Jesus Christ.

Habakkuk 2:1-3

I will stand upon my watch, and set me upon the tower, and will watch to see what he will say unto me, and what I shall answer when I am reproved. And the Lord answered me and said, write the vision, and make it plain upon tables, that he may run that readeth it. For the vision is yet for an appointed time, but at the end it shall speak, and not lie: thou it tarry, wait for it; because it will surely come, it will not tarry.

When we are developed sufficiently enough to handle the responsibility and accountability of the call, God will launch us into the place he has called us to walk in.

I Timothy 2:4

Who will have all men to be saved, and to come into the knowledge of the truth.

Chapter Eight

The Challenge Issued

Many people, saved and unsaved, have been told that God does not call women to preach the gospel and He definitely does not use women in the office of Pastor/Teacher. Regardless of what has been said and taught, each of us must examine the scriptures for ourselves and determine if the things we have been told can be verified in scripture. One of the greatest awakenings for me has been that much of what I learned in church (in years past) was not true and the greatest percentage came from those in leadership. The Holy Spirit is the Revealer of Truth. He is the "Interpreter of Truth" and if we are going to have an understanding of the plan of God, we must depend upon Him to open our eyes so that we may see. It is the responsibility of every believer to do more than just read scripture.

We must study the scriptures. **(II Timothy 2:15)** We must trust the Holy Spirit to illuminate our minds as we go through the Bible and lay aside our own opinions and the opinions of others. We must be willing to admit that much of the erroneous beliefs and misinterpretations of scriptures have governed our lives and behavior for years. We may have received information from people we highly respected, role models, mentors, or those we view as credible in their positions of authority. No matter how we received the information, it is quite possible that we need to examine the validity of the information received. We must be teachable because there is so much more to learn and all of us are ignorant in some areas of life. Nobody knows everything there is to know on a given topic.

It takes courage and humility to admit that we don't know everything, and that we could have made a mistake. The person who thinks he knows everything and never makes a mistake, is dangerous to himself and to others. Just because I have believed a thing for a long time and those before me believed it, does not make it truth. I could have believed a lie for years. For example, many believe that the thorn in Paul's flesh was sickness and disease; however, if one will carefully study the scriptures, the Bible clearly states what the thorn in the flesh was **(II Corinthians 12:7-12).**

Out of all that Paul mentions that he went through **(II Corinthians 11:23-27),** not one time does he mention being sick, having epilepsy, being hunchback or having fainting spells; yet the misinterpretation of this scripture has been perpetuated throughout generations because of the lack of study and man's inability to rightly divide the Word of Truth. It is also perpetuated by the Spirit of Error who comes to blind the eyes of man's understanding that he see not.

John 8:44

Ye are of your father the devil, and the lusts of your father ye will do. He was a murderer from the beginning, and abode not in the truth, because there is no truth in him. When he speaketh a lie, he speaketh of his own: for he is a liar, and the father of it.

II Corinthians 4:3-6

But if our gospel be hid, it is hid to them that are lost: in whom the god of this world hath blinded the minds of them which believe not, lest the light of the glorious gospel of Christ, who is the image of God, should shine unto them. For we preach not ourselves but Christ Jesus the Lord; and ourselves your servants for Jesus sake. For God, who commanded the light to shine out of darkness, hath shined in our hearts, to give the light of the knowledge of the glory of God in the face of Jesus Christ.

John 3:18-21

He that believeth on him is not condemned: but he that believeth not is condemned already, because he hath not believed in the name of the only begotten Son of God. And this is the condemnation, that light is come into the world, and men loved darkness rather than light, because their deeds were evil. For every one that doeth evil hateth the light, neither cometh to the light, lest his deeds should be reproved. But he that doth truth cometh to the light, that his deeds may be made manifest, that they are wrought in God.

Satan is the Spirit of Error and he is the father of lies. His objective is twofold. He attempts to keep the people of God from first of all, receiving knowledge and secondly, from receiving understanding. Without knowledge and understanding he can hold us in bondage. Consider the following scriptures:

Jeremiah 3:15

And I will give you pastors according to mine heart, which shall feed you with knowledge and understanding.

Jeremiah 33:3

Call unto me, and I will answer thee, and shew thee great and mighty things, which thou knowest not.

John 8:30-32

As he spake these words, many believed on him. Then said Jesus to those Jews which believed on him, if ye continue in my word, then are ye my disciples indeed; and ye shall know the truth, and the truth shall make you free.

Colossians 1:9-11

For this cause we also, since the day we heard it, do not cease to pray for you, and to desire that ye might be filled with the knowledge of his will in all wisdom and spiritual understanding; That ye might walk worthy of the Lord unto all pleasing, being fruitful in every good work, and increasing in the knowledge God; strengthened with all might, according to his glorious power, unto all patience and longsuffering with joyfulness;

Ephesians 1:10

Having made known unto us the mystery of His will, according to his good pleasure which he hath purposed in Himself.

My aim is not to go through every passage from which the above scriptures were taken to explain them in detail, but simply to allow every reader to see that it is God's will that we receive knowledge and understanding. In Colossians, we see the word "**wisdom**". Wisdom is the wherewithal to take acquired knowledge, coupled with understanding and properly implement it on a day to day basis. God's will is that the eyes of our understanding be flooded with light. What eyes? Not our physical eyes, but the eyes of our understanding spirit. He wants us to have full insight into His ways and purposes. Then and only then can we walk in total liberty, total freedom.

Ignorance is not an excuse, even though it has been used as an excuse. Ignorance simply means, unknowledgeable or unlearned. It is deadly and yet, equally as dangerous is one who hears the truth, can clearly discern the truth, but chooses to reject the truth they hear. It is like two men being locked in a jail cell; both have the keys to unlock the cell and experience freedom. One does not know that the key in his hand will bring him freedom and the other knows, but refuses to act on what he knows. Neither of the two will experience freedom, one because of ignorance, the other by choice.

Hosea 4:6

*My people are destroyed for a lack of knowledge:
because thou hast rejected knowledge, I will also
reject thee, that thou shall be no priest to me:
seeing thou has forgotten the law of thy God, I
will also forget thy children.*

God speaks of His people and He says, His people are destroyed because they don't know. But not only do they not know, but when truth is revealed, they reject truth. God says, when you reject truth, you are rejecting Him and if we reject God, He rejects us. When there is no relationship with God or knowledge of God, our children are deprived of the opportunity to know God and serve Him for themselves. I cannot emphasize enough that every believer has the responsibility of studying the scriptures. As God illuminates His Word to you concerning His will for women in ministry, you will be faced with new information; new in the sense that you have not known, not because it has not always been so. It will be left up to you to embrace the truths revealed or reject them. The choice is yours.

How do I change if I have been operating on false information? The first thing I must do is, find out what the truth is. After I find truth, I receive it, and embrace it, by making it a vital part of my life. When I am introduced to truth, and refuse to change, I set myself in concert with the forces of darkness and perpetuate a misrepresentation of scripture. I can excuse my actions and attempt to justify myself before men. An excuse is a lie told to justify my unwillingness to change.

Adhering to the truth affords every man the opportunity to live life to the maximum. Too many of us have allowed lies to be perpetuated in this earth. Whether intentional or unintentional, if I believe a thing is true, even though it is a lie, it is the truth to me. Truth is based upon the evidence of the original principle. Jesus is truth and His Word is the evidence of the original principle, plan, and purpose for every person walking planet earth, whether male or female. When we don't acknowledge the truth, we will always be in bondage to a lie.

TO WRITE OR RECEIVE ADDITIONAL INFORMATION
FROM
DR. JAQUELINE T. FLOWERS

WRITE TO:

TIME OF CELEBRATION MINISTRIES CHURCH
C/O DR. JACQUELINE T. FLOWERS
P. O. BOX 671522
HOUSTON, TEXAS 77267-1522
(832) 237-2400 – OFFICE
(832) 237-2410 - FAX

Made in the USA
Columbia, SC
16 September 2024

41853833R00074